A dawn-to-dusk manual for
living effortlessly and elegantly
in the modern world

 Thames & Hudson

FOREWORD

When we launched MR PORTER in February 2011, our goal was to bring style to men all over the world in the most easy, natural and effortless manner possible. Now, here we are, nearly 10 years later, with a book – the one you're holding in your hands – that purports to have all the answers, not just when it comes to your wardrobe, but your entire life (albeit, over a 24-hour period). "Goodness," you might be thinking. Or, yes, "How dare they?"

The truth, of course, is that there is no single tome out there that can straighten out all the kinks in a man's life, or even a single day of it. Nonetheless, what we at MR PORTER have realised, over many years of compiling features and practical how-to guides, and talking to some of the world's most interesting and thoroughly well-put-together men, is that we now have enough helpful tips, tricks and insights at our fingertips to provide dawn-to-dusk coverage when it comes to helping men do things just ever so slightly better. So, we thought, why shouldn't we?

The result of this thought experiment is not so much an instruction manual (though its "How To" inserts might be formatted like one) or a set of commandments (though you might do worse than follow its precepts) as it is an encyclopaedic buffet of ideas that will, hopefully, lessen the sting of even the most mundane and onerous of your diurnal rituals. Whether it encourages you to make drastic changes, such as setting your alarm to the same time as fashion designer Mr Tom Ford (spoiler: it is early), or simple ones, such as improving your domestic lighting situation, making better eggs for breakfast, or booking your next holiday like a seasoned globetrotter – the point of it all is purely to aid you through the day with a little extra helping of... what's the word? Ah, yes, *enjoyment.*

On that subject, we're well aware that every day needs a bit of fun to it, which is why, alongside the useful, we've made sure to include plenty within these pages that you might describe as not *just* useful, but also "thoughtful" or "wistful" or "playful". This is partially in service of presenting you with a more enjoyable reading experience, while part of the thinking behind it is to underline the fact that, life, at the end of the day, doesn't always need to be so serious. Consider internalising this sentiment as step one of your quest towards a better day. Step two is easy: just turn the page...

Alongside keeping the world's men stylish, promoting their wellbeing and happiness is one of MR PORTER's key ambitions. As such, we have launched Health In Mind, a fund and content initiative dedicated to helping men feel better. Find out more at *mrporter.com/health-in-mind*

1 RISE AND SHINE

2 THE FIT FACTOR

3 BETTER GROOMING

4 SMARTER WORKING

5 HEALTH IN MIND

6   NOURISHMENT

7   STEPPING OUT

8   STAYING IN

9   GOING PLACES

1

WHAT SUCCESSFUL MEN EAT FOR BREAKFAST

Start the day as you mean to go on...

Words by Mr Stuart Husband

"Eat breakfast like a king, lunch like a prince, and dinner like a pauper," runs the old saying, and it is one that many of the world's most successful men, on the evidence listed overleaf, have taken to heart. It seems that the road to greatness is lined with early morning chow-downs comprising everything from coffee and cucumbers to the occasional Class A drug. Rise – and shine!

Mr Elvis Presley eating a sandwich, Memphis, 1958

MR JACK DORSEY *co-founder, Twitter; founder, Square*

Who needs breakfast?
The Twitter CEO and co-founder refrains from eating breakfast at all for much of the week. Instead, he favours a 22-hour fast, which means he only eats dinner. Clearly, there is room for only so many feeds in one's life.

MR ELVIS PRESLEY *singer*

The "Elvis Sandwich"
Mr Presley's preference for junk food reached landfill proportions with his legendary breakfast sandwich, which consisted of a pair of fried bread wedges slathered in butter, peanut butter, honey, three rashers of bacon and half a banana, doubtless leaving his digestive tract "All Shook Up".

MR MARK WAHLBERG *actor*

Blueberries, eggs, turkey burgers and a protein shake
If one is eating at 2.30am, it is usually because of a mis-judged trip to a late-night eatery. But this is Mr Wahlberg's breakfast time. He starts with "oats, peanut butter, blueberries and eggs," then a protein shake, three turkey burgers and sweet potatoes. Healthier than a cheeseburger, right?

MR WH AUDEN *poet*

Benzedrine and a crossword
What inspired Mr Auden to poetic heights such as "Funeral Blues"? He apparently rose shortly after 6.00am, made coffee, grappled with *The Times* crossword – and took a dose of Benzedrine, after which the stanzas came thick and (super) fast.

MR NELSON MANDELA *political leader*

Eggs and bacon
Breakfast wasn't always a great meal for the late South African president and political prisoner. In 1988, after treatment for tuberculosis, he was served a plate of bacon and eggs, which the doctor advised him not to have. His response? He would eat his breakfast, even if it killed him.

MR KEITH RICHARDS *guitarist, The Rolling Stones*

A joint

For the majority of people, the idea of a joint for breakfast would be somewhat hardcore; for Mr Keith Richards, it's positively lightweight. Yes, The Rolling Stones guitarist enjoys an early morning toke, but there was a time when his "full English" consisted of a heroin/cocaine cocktail.

MR LEBRON JAMES *basketball player*

Fruity Pebbles

For his morning cereal, the NBA superstar chooses Fruity Pebbles, which is full of nutritious, well, rice, we suppose? Mr James even designed his Nike Lebron 15 "Fruity Pebbles" in homage to his favourite repast.

MR WOLFGANG AMADEUS MOZART *composer*

Chicken legs with sour cream and potatoes

Before knocking out a piano sonata, Mr Mozart would sit down to half a capon with fried onions, garlic and smoked paprika, served with potatoes and sour cream. Maybe that was why 18th-century critics were wont to dismiss his output as "overloaded and overstuffed"?

MR LUCIAN FREUD *painter*

Milky Earl Grey, pains aux raisins, nougat

The artist attended the same restaurant for breakfast, Clarke's, in Kensington, for 15 years, sitting at the same table, and ordering the same things: an excessively milky Earl Grey tea, pains au raisin or porridge, and a bar of nougat to appease his famously sweet tooth.

MR FERGUS HENDERSON *chef and founder, St John*

Espresso, Fernet Branca and (perhaps) a cigarette

The bon vivant founder of St John opts for an espresso, a glass of Fernet Branca and a cigarette. "It fires up the engine, and improves the humours," he told *Vanity Fair* in 2010. Then, in 2016, he announced that he now omitted the cigarette, which seems a wise choice.

Mr Lucian Freud with his mother, Ms Lucie Freud, at the Sagne Coffee Shop
on Marylebone High Street, London, circa 1980

WHY MR TOM FORD GETS UP EARLIER THAN YOU

Words by Mr Jeremy Langmead

The tricky thing about interviewing Mr Tom Ford is trying to come up with a new way to conduct it. He's done it all: he's answered almost every intimate question you could imagine asking; chatted nude with *The Sunday Times*' Mr AA Gill, and, for another feature, posed in the buff with two models in the shower. He has nothing to hide. What you see is what you get: an enormously successful and driven designer and businessman who's also absurdly charming, handsome, amusing, self-deprecating and, of course, stylish. All in all, rather intimidating.

It turns out, thankfully, that he does have one or two weaknesses. He doesn't sleep well. Although he is careful with his waist – usually eating just sushi for lunch – he does have a predilection for Colin the Caterpillar fruit gums. "My assistants think I don't like people who eat," he laughs. "It's true I don't like to see or smell food in the office. But I don't like the staff to leave the office, either. I've never actually seen anyone here eat. Perhaps they eat under their desks when I'm in here doing interviews."

He leads a healthy existence these days – no alcohol, few carbs, early nights – partly because he's getting older, but mostly because he's a father, and that takes a lot of energy. Being a parent means he has relaxed about some aspects of his life – house not as tidy as it was, grooming regimen no longer as elaborate – but you wouldn't know. His office is immaculate; his hair perfect, his facial stubble ink-black (he has help with the latter, he admits, as he's not yet ready to be a silver daddy).

One word that has always been associated with Mr Ford is "sex". Has fatherhood had any impact on that? Short answer: yes.

"I feel less sexy now that I'm a father – and, actually, there's a scientific reason for that," he says. "I read that men who are the primary caregivers of children have lower testosterone levels. It drops, according to some reports, because nature wants the man to stay with the children and not let them wander off... Now I don't know if my testosterone levels have dropped or not, I haven't had them tested, but I feel less sexy, definitely.

"I suppose stopping drinking made me feel less sexy, too," he adds, unprompted. "I think that being drunk all the time used to fuel, and I don't mean my sex drive, but my... you know, I did a lot of things with [risqué fashion photographer] Terry Richardson, that I wouldn't have otherwise done." He's referring to the aforementioned shower shoot.

"I was a highly functioning alcoholic," he says. "I think I did a lot of things creatively that I probably wouldn't have done had I been sober. In the end, they kind of all worked to my advantage."

He sobered up after leaving the Gucci group in 2004, launching TOM FORD cosmetics, fragrance and eyewear, writing and directing an award-winning movie, *A Single Man*, and unveiling his own menswear label. This, from the beginning, has been aimed at a jet-set customer who appreciates not only how his clothes look, but how they feel and fit. The tailoring is classic yet distinctive – wide pointed lapels, a fitted waist – and the sportswear so tactile and covetable that when you travel, you want to book it in a seat next to you rather than check it in.

One imagines Mr Ford spends a long time getting ready each morning. But while he wakes early at around 4.30am, it's due to an inability to sleep rather than a need to preen. "I get up and make myself a gigantic iced coffee," he says. "I then answer emails and work until about 6.00am. Then I will head upstairs and have a second giant iced coffee and lay in the bathtub. I don't like warm drinks of any kind. I lay in my bathtub with a bendable straw in my coffee and no lights and only one candle lit. I love that time in the morning when no one else is awake, and I'm alone, and then I can slowly come to life."

He insists his grooming regimen is often low-maintenance. "Today, because I was having an interview, it consisted of trimming my beard." After that, he says, he gets dressed and wakes up his son, Jack, at 7.30am. "Richard [his husband, Mr Buckley] and I have breakfast with our son until about 9.00am and then I leave for the office."

Evenings, too, are now equally low-key. If Mr Ford has to socialise, he tries to be home in bed by midnight at the latest. If he isn't going out, he's apparently in bed watching TV by 10.00pm. "Talk about unsexy," he says. I'm not sure many would agree.

WHERE TO FIND THE BEST COFFEE SHOPS ON THE PLANET

From the Americas to Scandinavia to Australia, here are the places to get a damn fine cup of joe

Words by Mr Will Dean

THE COFFEE COLLECTIVE *Copenhagen*

After starting as a warehouse roaster, The Coffee Collective now has four locations in Copenhagen, but the Jægersborggade venue might just be the finest. It's designed to look like an apartment, with staff serving you from the kitchen. The interiors are slick and good-looking, and the staff are, too. Here, simple wooden furniture in Scandi greys and whites is given a boost of colour by huge portraits of the people who farmed the beans.

Pop in for a stunning flat white. Perhaps stay for the barista courses or coffee-tasting classes on offer. And on the first Friday of the month, the team behind it offer a tour of the Frederiksberg roastworks.

Jægersborggade 57, 2200 Copenhagen. coffeecollective.dk

The Coffee Collective, Bernikow, Copenhagen

ONIBUS COFFEE *Tokyo*

Tokyo is a city full of Starbucks-like chains (and plenty of actual Starbucks), but speciality roasters and indies have been creeping into the mainstream for a while now. Onibus Coffee owner Mr Sakao Atsushi was inspired by a trip to Australia in his mid-twenties where he witnessed the rising third-wave artisanal coffee culture. Upon his return to Tokyo, Mr Atsushi decided to open his own roastworks and serving window, followed by this Nakameguro café in an old *okayu* (rice porridge) restaurant. It has become a haven for both commuters and an easy-going family crowd keen for a single-origin espresso and a comfortable, pared-back place to pause.

2 Chome-14-1 Kamimeguro, Meguro City, Tokyo. onibuscoffee.com

CAFFÈ AL BICERIN *Turin*

Caffè Al Bicerin reeks of history. You can sit at the favourite table of Mr Camillo Benso di Cavour, unified Italy's first prime minister, while philosopher Mr Friedrich Nietzsche also drank here. In fact, the place has been serving Torino's signature brew, *bicerin*, since 1763. A rich hot chocolate with an added layer of espresso and fresh cream, the drink was named after the glass it still is served in. With much still the same as it was in the 1800s, this is no *rapido* espresso joint. It is a place to linger and to drink in the history, maybe with a slice of *torta di nocciole*.

Piazza della Consolata, 5, 10122 Torino. bicerin.it

DROP COFFEE *Stockholm*

Drop Coffee began life as a small coffee bar with a one-kiln bean roaster in 2009. Three years later, it opened a separate roaster with 25 times the capacity and was supplying Java to some of the world's finest coffee shops. The reason for this rapid growth? Well, Swedes love coffee, and Drop Coffee just so happens to roast the best brew in the country.

In the Mariatorget café, Bolivian, Colombian, El Salvadorian, Ethiopian and Kenyan beans, all supplied directly from the farmers, are brewed to perfection in a venue that drips with Scandinavian cool. Go there for breakfast, lunch or *fika*.

Wollmar Yxkullsgatan 10, 118 50 Stockholm. dropcoffee.com

Onibus Coffee, Nakameguro, Tokyo

Previous page: Single O, Surry Hills, Sydney.
This page: Barista Parlor, Germantown, Nashville

SINGLE O *Sydney*

Opened in Surry Hills in 2003, Single O has since expanded to include a roastworks out in Botany (which sells wholesale), a streetside bar in the central business district and, interestingly, a roastery and tasting bar in Tokyo. If that doesn't give you a sense of its ambition, then how about its involvement in the invention of The Juggler, a chilled milk-dispensing system that does away with fiddling around with plastic bottles?

Suffice to say, having an ethical supply line is treated seriously. As is the environment. The roastworks runs on solar power and Single O runs free coffee schemes in a bid to tackle the scourge of paper coffee cups.

Various locations Sydney (and Tokyo). singleo.com.au

EIGHTFOLD COFFEE *Los Angeles*

Minimalist, good-looking, cool and arty, Eightfold fits right in in Echo Park, one of Los Angeles' hippest boroughs. Its owner, Ms Soo Kim, came here from New York with a pedigree for design rather than hot beverages. That much is obvious from the wooden open shelves and the marble serving counter, but the coffee, exclusively from Portland's revered Heart Roasters, is great, too. Meanwhile, the café's name comes from the eight stages of self-discovery in Mr Hermann Hesse's *Siddhartha*. The last stage is concentration, and this is the perfect place for that.

1294 Sunset Blvd, Los Angeles. eightfoldcoffee.com

BARISTA PARLOR *Nashville*

Opened in 2011, Barista Parlor has rapidly become Nashville's most lauded coffee house. Art plays a big role. A huge mural by local artist Mr Bryce McCloud hangs over the room, the centrepiece of which is a magnificent handmade Slayer espresso machine. And that's before you get to the coffees, which come from some of the best roasters in the US and change daily. Everything else, from the staff uniforms and aprons to the ceiling lights and the sausage in the biscuit, is sourced locally.

Barista Parlor's other outposts include a collaboration with The Black Keys' Mr Dan Auerbach in the old Golden Sound recording studios.

Various locations, Nashville. baristaparlor.com

WHY GETTING DRESSED IS A LIFELONG PROCESS

MR PORTER's man in New York digs deep after a major wardrobe upheaval and the soul-searching it prompted

Words by Mr Chris Wallace

This may sound crazy, especially for someone who has worked as an editor at fashiony magazines for more than a decade, but I'm not really that into clothes. Tell the truth, I probably think about style less than you. And *fashion*? I've never met him. Even that most fundamental interaction with clothes – getting dressed in the morning – is a blur. All I want is to wear something that makes me feel like the person I tell myself I am, and then not to think about it again for the rest of the day.

To that point, what I am interested in, more so than anything else, is identity – mine and just about everyone else's – who we are, who we project ourselves to be, all those characters that we play. And, of course, clothes are the best way of getting into character. They are the best way of exteriorising our taste, of signifying values. In that way, anyway, clothes really do maketh the man.

But what happens to you, your self and past selves if your clothes... disappear? Not by any wilful, Ms Marie Kondo-style exorcism, but suddenly, in one moment and for evermore, they simply vanish? Like, gone-gone. From one day to the next, 10-year-old denim, gone. Gone, the bespoke suits. Gone, the unmentionables. The accessories, the sentimental oddities. Gone. Gone – the clothes you've worn to be all the versions of yourself you've ever known, the only sort of memorabilia of your 40 years on Earth. Poof! Gone.

Last year, after a bit of a rough break-up and a move so long and dreary that Sir David Lean would've found it boring, I finally opened up my bags to find that I was missing, well, just about everything. Suffice to say that, when we split, I was in a rush to get gone and my ex was eager to have every piece of me deleted from the scene. Ergo gone. Everything gone. Everything but the very core, the clothes I'd set aside to wear during the move, the clothes that were close at hand, the most durable – a pair of Levi's, a pair of Red Wings, a few sweaters and my Rick Owens jackets. A good core, the kind of garments you could wear through any sort of apocalypse, even one a little more severe than my petty, personal Ragnarök. But a repertoire maybe a tad *essentialist* for a modern metropolitan life. Prohibitively so, in fact.

So, to shop. But where even to begin when one needs everything? There is no real beginning to any wardrobe, but in this instance there was a ticking clock of necessity to act as my guide. During the dread middle of winter in New York, the first thing I needed was a coat. I have somewhat ironically always been a buy-it-once-buy-it-for-life guy, wanting only pieces that will outlive me, or at least accompany me for as long as I require them, which has tended to hamper explorations into flash and trend. To be honest, I've always been slightly cautious of even marginally directional clothing, feeling more comfortable in trad classics. And yet I'd grown very used to wearing my Rick, so the coat I got was a wild cloak from Mr Owens, and I think I wore it every day for the rest of the season. I loved it beyond mention.

I loved it more than most of the other things that had survived the great purge, in fact, and so it inspired me to edit still further. If I was going to be so deliberate about what was in my wardrobe, I thought, shouldn't I subject everything to the same rigorous selection process? (Maybe the new me was an athletic goth?) And so, my belongings grew even lighter still as I threw out bad T-shirts after good suits, light enough that they could all fit into a single Rimowa cabin-friendly suitcase, light enough that I could see the entire collection from a bird's eye view and think about them in toto. Which led me to wonder, if the clothes make the man and I can begin my wardrobe again from the beginning, who in the world was I supposed to be?

"The challenge of modern freedom, or the combination of isolation and freedom which confronts you," writes Mr Saul Bellow's narrator in *Ravelstein*, "is to make yourself up." Whole cloth, as they say. From scratch. Which we do (or at least I have to do) every morning, every time we dress ourselves up to greet the world, whether we are dressing to suit a mood or suit an occasion. My re-wardrobing situation felt like that daily application of identity on magic mushrooms – all of my choices seemed over-fraught, overly meaningful, definitive in a way that made me terribly uncomfortable, but also incredibly intrigued. Just think of the potential mes dwelling in all those unbought clothes.

Walking around Mayfair in London on a work trip, I started shopping for identities the way others were shopping for brollies and whatnot. Look at those elegant gentlemen walking around in hoary old Anderson & Sheppard suits and their George Cleverley shoes, looking like latter-day Sir John Gielguds. Isn't that who I've always aspired to be? Or am I, at heart, just the same jocky Angeleno kid I was in long-sleeve Stüssy tees, baggy shorts and tie-dye socks? Or what of this seemingly louche former spy now working in a late-night casino – all Haider Ackermann everything – *no need to wrap it up, I'll wear it out.*

And so on, ad insanium, until I'd frightened myself into a kind of stagnation. Thinking of every option, every me available on the shop rack, I was too overwhelmed, too afraid to commit to any one personality for fear of something like existential buyer's remorse. Every morning I would wake up and have to reboot myself, installing seemingly new software of beliefs and behaviours the same way I was putting on my T-shirts and jeans – half-heartedly. But still, life made its demands regularly. I had a hiking trip, a beach trip, a ski trip and a fancy dinner to equip myself for. Inaction wasn't an option, but the idea of shopping seemed like science fiction. So, instead of moving forwards, I went back in time, pulling up old #tbt pictures to see if, maybe, the direction in which I ought to be headed might not have already been set forth by the various mes I'd dressed up as in the past.

It turns out that when I was a kid, I loved dressing up. Looking back at pictures of the clothes I wore between the ages of, say, five and 15, it's as if every day was Halloween and I really loved outfitting myself as the characters I wished to be. In kindergarten, I wore the silver lamé-like onesie I'd gotten on a trip to the Kennedy Space Center for, like, a month straight. Then there was the *Return Of The Jedi*-era Luke Skywalker look – black cotton hoodies and kimono robes with my bowl-cut mop. On vacation with my dad in New Mexico in the late 1980s, I dressed like a cowboy, replete with full bolo tie and 10-gallon hat. By the beach in my teens, I wore puka shells around my neck. As a skater in junior high, it was acid-washed denim and oversized logo T-shirts. There were costumes everywhere, as far as I looked.

But, more even than my apparent Zelig-like attempts to melt into a scene, to disappear into a world as if I were meant to be there, as if I belonged, my childhood dressing-up was, I think, an attempt to try on personality traits and types, to discern which might fit best. (Which, on reflection, made complete sense, coming as it was from someone who spent years writing a novel called *The Chameleon* about a man who shapeshifts to fit into whichever milieu he finds himself.) Unsure of whom I was, or could be, I suppose I was shopping for facets of me-ness. Perhaps I imagined that if I at least got in costume as every passing character I found appealing, I might pick up a few keepsakes by way of style, personality and behaviour that would better equip me to face the world. And I'm not sure that process of trial and error has ever really stopped. I've just gotten older and lazier.

In my more recent pictures (of the past 10 years or so), the outfits I'm wearing break down into three distinct styles, three characters. First, there is the workaday classic man wearing what Mr Andy Warhol called the "editor's uniform" of dark blazer, Oxford shirt and jeans, which mostly made me look like your seventh-grade history teacher. Then there is what I might've imagined to be Han Solo off duty, but rendered me closer to Villain #6 in a bad Mr Nicolas Cage movie – Henley shirt, leather jacket, jeans and boots. The last is my James-Bond-on-vacation scenario – Hawaiian shirts and linen things – in which I ended up resembling Bond's far less cool quartermaster, Q, going incognito.

Not exactly a bravura style performance and still, as I began to piece my wardrobe back together, I found that I continued to hew towards that trio. I was rebuying the wardrobe I'd by chance stolen my escape

from – again with the Henleys and dark denim, again into the tailored clothing and again, for my sins, heavy on Hawaiian shirts. It was with a kind of doomed disappointment that I figured that these specific threads ran through my taste like electromagnetic lay lines, that I was always destined to tend towards these poles.

I was made even more acutely aware of my re-outfitting conundrum by, first, working alongside a slew of clotheshorses at a men's lifestyle magazine, but also by simply existing in New York City, the American capital of vanity and self-importance, where so much of our self-branding and personal self-worth is projected by both our person and our style. At several points, these competing pressures made me want to throw up my hands, to just opt out. Tees and jeans for ever. The world be damned.

But there were moments when I made some sort of headway, moments during shopping or stock taking of my incrementally expanding wardrobe, when I was able to recognise certain items as being essentially me. There were, for example, things that I had learned about myself and which manifested in preferences for particular pieces of clothing. For knobbly, woven textures on my suits, to make a bad example, or for brown suede boots above all other shoes, to make a better one. Even more specifically, at my current rate of travel – at least twice a month – I go through security a lot and I've found that, within the genus of suede boots, I prefer the species chukka and desert for travel days (soft, few lace holes so that they go through metal detectors easily and go off and on simply if needs be). So, progress, right?

Well, in keeping with tradition, every time I have taken a step forwards, towards understanding my style and taste – and thus understanding myself – I have spiralled backwards like a poked balloon. And this last, most recent time was probably the worst and most comprehensive. Even as I was making tiny, somewhat specific choices about socks or shirts or whatever, it began to dawn on me that I was getting no closer to any sort of real me-ness. What sort of identity is it to choose option A from four similar options in a multiple-choice question? Where, in there, is anything that we have come to understand about style, about character and personality? Again, the urge came to just disappear from the world of clothes, to vanish the way a man in a grey flannel suit might have vanished in the 1950s. Of course, a grey flannel suit is no longer the grey flannel suit of metaphor. If I wore that to the office, let alone to a dinner party, everyone would ask me why I was so dressed up. How now to get away? How to both disappear into our contemporary world *and disappear into myself*?

Then, with a kind of revelation, a kind of epiphany, I came, in my search through old pictures, onto a period in my twenties when I was living in Los Angeles, during and after graduate school, working in a restaurant and making short films, in which I dressed in a uniform of Goodwill suits with jazzy shirts and sneakers. Right away, I remembered feeling entirely at home in those clothes. I was dressed up enough to go into any scenario (and not be asked about it tediously), yet casual enough to be me, specific and referential enough to make me feel like I was in a conversation with the characters whom I aspired to be. I was in communion with the many mes I hoped to be playing.

And as soon as I had that revelation, this feeling of comfort – of exaltation, really, of discovering this moment in time – I felt another, nearer chime. Sitting in my office, looking at those old photographs, I was wearing almost the exact same clothes. The suits were a bit nicer now, the jazzy shirts were made by Dries Van Noten, but here I was again, dressed, for the first time, just like myself.

It wasn't exactly the kind of revelation that cures all present and potential worries (the student loans are still there and I still lack a good safari jacket and chef's knife), but it was the kind of clouds-parting pause that made me feel like the decisions to come, the existential crises ahead would be a little less severe. The next morning, as I dressed, in what I now teased myself was my signature look, I started thinking of other things, everything else, in fact. And now I can happily never think about it again. At least, that is, until the fall.

HOW TO COOK EGGS LIKE AN EXPERT

Words by Mr Adam Welch

When it comes to cooking, eggs are usually among the first ingredients you need to get to grips with, but can also be the most difficult to master. The fact that different people like their eggs cooked in different ways tends to complicate this matter even further. Given that we face up to the things pretty much every weekend at brunch, we thought it smart to seek out the best methods for cooking them. Though there are plenty of chefs out there, all with their own philosophies and methods, it's hard to imagine that many have spent more time thinking about eggs and their applications than Mr Nick Korbee, executive chef at New York's Egg Shop. Opened in 2014, the original Nolita hotspot was initially intended to offer the perfect egg sandwich. However, when experimentation started, it was clear that they could do a lot more with the humble ingredient.

"Everybody has some emotional connection to an egg, to eating an egg, to cooking an egg," says Mr Korbee. "And that's why it's an amazing ingredient. When you say 'egg', I immediately think of the perfect soft scrambled egg that my grandmother used to make for me and put over white toast. And it was just so simple but, you know, if I stubbed my toe and started crying, that's all I wanted to eat." Here, Mr Korbee offers his expert guide to cooking them in all our favourite ways: that is, boiled, poached, scrambled and fried. Once you've got these techniques sorted, avoid what Mr Korbee calls "the stigma of any style" with his tips to take your eggs that one step further.

POACHING

"Poaching is easier than you would think. First, you need a saucepan – not a frying pan, skillet, stock pot, or brassier, just a basic saucepan. Fill the pan at least ¾ full with hot water and bring it to a rapid simmer with 4 tbsp cider vinegar, and 1 tbsp sea salt. By rapid simmer, I mean Jacuzzi-level swirl and bubbles (the point just before, in a real Jacuzzi, you turn on the jets and get weird). Next, smoothly release the egg into the poach-cuzzi. You can either risk the nerve endings in your fingertips by cracking the egg and releasing it directly on the surface of the water, or you can crack it into any small vessel and pour it in to the water.

The egg will initially sink, but the motion of the bubbles in the water will turn the egg for you, so there is no need to stir. Using a slotted spoon, check the egg after about 2 minutes by gently lifting it to the surface. Go ahead: poke it with your finger. If it's not fully set, throw it back in and check again in a hot 30 seconds."

The extra mile
"Poach a dozen quail eggs and stuff each of them in the round of an avocado. It's visually stunning, the flavour profile is similar across the ingredients and it builds your timing skills as well."

FRYING

"A fried egg can be prepared sunny side up, over easy/medium/hard, or crispy (the new darling of fried-egg preparation). My preferred sunny-side-up style is prepared over medium-low heat in a non-stick or cast-iron pan with a minimal amount of canola/rapeseed oil. When the pan is up to temperature – when you can only hold your hand over it for 15 seconds before it gets too hot – add a tiny bit of oil, swirl to coat the pan, crack the egg into it, and turn the heat to low. The egg should not sputter and bubble out of control and the white should begin to set immediately. Once it has set on the bottom, after about 1 minute, give the unset white near the yolk a little poke with a spatula or wooden spoon. This should cause any raw white to spread out and cook a bit faster.

"To go over easy through hard, do the same thing as described above except flip the egg instead of poking at the unset white. To practice this in a sauté pan, test your skills on a slice of bread or another similarly weighted flat object that you don't mind throwing on the floor repeatedly.

"To make your eggs crispy, simply add more oil or fat, and keep the heat at medium-low until you have achieved your desired level of Insta-ready golden-brownness (this should take about 4 or 5 minutes). Remember: if you turn the heat up high, you will likely burn the bottom of the egg before it gets crispy."

The extra mile
"Try basting the eggs, until the white on top is set, with butter or with whatever oil you're using. Or, to avoid a flipping disaster, cover the pan to steam the eggs for a similar effect."

BOILING

"For boiled eggs, there are just a few rules and timings to remember. First, there should be enough boiling water to cover the eggs by one inch. Next, you must have an ice bath prepared for the second your eggs are ready to be removed from the water. Don't half-ass this by running cold tap water over the eggs, popping them in the fridge or some other such nonsense. When you are ready to cook, ie, your water is boiling, carefully lower the eggs into the pan, being sure not to crack the shells. I use a slotted spoon for just a few eggs and a spider/pasta strainer when working with large batches. For soft yolks, I remove the eggs to an ice bath after 6 minutes. For my perfect hard-boiled yolk, which is just a little under a true 'hard' texture, I remove the eggs after 10 minutes. If you leave them for a full 12 minutes, you've sunk your

battleship, and the yolk will be as grey as a navy destroyer. Wait until the eggs are fully cool to the touch before peeling under gently running water."

The extra mile
"Boiled eggs are great because after boiling, you can peel them or even just lightly crack the shell before letting them steep in any sort of bouillon or brine – both to colour the white and to add flavour to the eggs. I put them in with my pickled beetroots, which turns them a rich purple colour. The longer they stay in there the more the tone will sink in, so after long enough, you'll have vibrant purple 'white' all the way through to the bright yellow yolk, which is beautiful."

SCRAMBLING

"Scrambling is stylistic. The French do it one way, Americans do it another, and at Egg Shop, we have our own technique of folding and shaping scrambled eggs particularly for perfect sandwiches. Whichever way you roll, it's important to incorporate some fat, whether it's heavy cream, sour cream, crème fraîche, yoghurt or butter. Aim for 1 tbsp fat per 2 eggs. In the case of heavy cream, you should incorporate it when you scramble the eggs. With anything else, you fold it in close to the end of the cooking process, when the pan is off the heat. For soft, creamy scrambled eggs, work over a medium-low heat in a non-stick pan, and stir gently and consistently. Only add salt at the end of the cooking process, as adding it at the beginning can draw water from the eggs and result in a weird broken curd situation."

The extra mile
"Don't sell yourself short. Try to look up as many methods as you possibly can, and work with them so it's not just a mush of scrambled eggs on a plate. I like to add a pinch of cayenne pepper with the salt, and the tiniest bit of fresh grated nutmeg in the winter time for that warm and fuzzy brunch-in-a-ski-lodge feeling."

Egg Shop: The Cookbook (William Morrow & Company) by Mr Nick Korbee is available now

How to:

GET DRESSED IN
THE MORNING

There is one question we are always asked: what are the clothes every man needs in his wardrobe? The answer, of course, varies depending on what you do, where you live and your personality. But we do like to help out where we can. So, here we go. Stock up on the essentials overleaf and you won't ever be caught out.

THE GROUND RULES

Pick it out the night before

The most important of all truths about morning dressing is that it starts 12 hours before you need to be out the door. By making your clothing selection the previous evening, you will not only have the time to make better, more considered choices, you'll also afford yourself a few precious extra minutes in bed.

Think through the day

Your outfit has to last all day, so plan for it. What's the weather going to be like? What meetings do you have at work? What are you doing after? It might sound obvious, but if you make a point of asking yourself these questions, you won't end up wearing your favourite do-not-wash shirt to an Italian restaurant, or your expletive-strewn Vetements hoodie to your first meeting with a new client. And that is a good thing.

Focus on neutrals

Keep your wardrobe well-stocked with neutral shades – that is, garments that are white, black, beige or navy. All these colours go together and with other colours (even navy and black; just make sure the navy is light enough to provide a contrast), and can be mixed with wild abandon, taking much of the thought out of the whole process.

Tone it down to two

If you do want to add colour, do it with restraint. In our decade of sartorial experiments, we at MR PORTER have discovered that most good outfits contain at most two main colours, in a 70:30 ratio. The leeway here is tonal variation. Light blue with dark blue with midnight blue, for example, still reads as blue, so you could afford a splash of red, pink or brown if you're looking to make things a little more interesting.

Watch your mouth

Don't go anywhere near your clothes until *after* you have brushed your teeth. Do we really need to tell you why?

THE DETAILS

The Oxford shirt

These shirts, which usually come in a thick textured cotton with button-down collars, are perfect for most day-to-day casual and smart-casual situations. Three is a good number to start with: one white, one light blue and one in a subtle pattern such as a Bengal stripe or microcheck.

The merino-wool crew neck

If you're feeling fancy, you could swap this for cashmere. But merino – a breathable, moisture-wicking fibre – is a little better at adapting to the seasons. Navy is always a safe bet, but, as outer layers tend to be darker, you'll also get a lot of use out of a brightly coloured variation here. Try orange, or even pink, if you're feeling brave.

The coat

A single breasted, knee-length coat in grey, black or navy can be worn in almost any situation. If you're looking to make it a bit more fun... maybe don't. A colourful scarf can do much work to this end, and won't carve quite as big a hole in your bank account as whatever patterned or embroidered thing you've got your eye on.

The umbrella

We're big fans of waterproof coats, but for an essentials-only wardrobe, an umbrella will suffice to keep you dry. Plus, if you get a hand-crafted example from the likes of Italian craftsman Mr Francesco Maglia, it can also make you look rather sophisticated.

The "dress" sneakers

Yes, sneakers can be smart. Indeed, they have become the modern era's most multi-purpose shoe, if chosen rightly. The typical example in this department the high-end tennis shoe, a style currently offered by every brand from Common Projects to Givenchy to John Lobb. Keep them sparkling white with a protective spray and Jason Markk's sneaker wipes.

2

THE FIT FACTOR

LULULEMON: THE FITNESS BRAND DESIGNED FOR REAL LIFE

Designer Mr Ben Stubbington
on creating sportswear that looks
good in and out of the gym

Words by Mr Chris Wallace

Y ou grow up in England," says Mr Ben Stubbington, senior vice president of men's design at lululemon, "and it's very much team sports, football. For some reason, that was never my thing. Maybe it's because I didn't love school and it was more about running away, and running away from people at that point, but I ended up getting into running, and into cycling – the road riding I do now."

From his hometown of Portsmouth, Mr Stubbington ran as far as the University of Brighton, where he studied fashion and print design. And from there to the US in the early 2000s, where he worked at Banana Republic and Calvin Klein, before becoming men's creative director at Theory, a post he held for seven years.

Still, he kept running. But in 2007, when Mr Stubbington was 27, while training for the New York City Marathon, he discovered an egg-sized growth behind one of his knees. The growth proved benign – but the surgery to remove it was less so. He was left with extensive nerve damage in his leg and even given slim chances of ever walking again – let alone running long distances. The physical therapy to get him back on his feet, he says, was gruelling. "I was very sick for a long time, and the only reason I walk today is because my mind was strong enough to power myself through. I had to rebuild my body," he says. "A lot of that was done through weights, TRX and things like that. But from there I found yoga as part of the process of healing, trying to create balance in my body, but also in my mind. I got into meditation as well," he says. "And I think when you get into these high-endurance activities, that's where you click into [the zone]."

Nowadays, the "flow state" is a principle pursuit of Mr Stubbington's, whether it's through yoga and meditation, surfing or in his art – oil on canvas. "My personal artwork is very close to what I get from sport or these activities we're talking about," he says, "which is this level of flow and reliance on self and this inner drive. And that's very separate from what I do with work. My design work, whether here at lululemon or past companies, is about finding a real equilibrium and working with a team."

Mr Stubbington joined the team at lululemon towards the end of 2016, relocating from New York to Vancouver where the company is based, and immediately fell for the Endor-like environment of the Pacific Northwest, where he cycles to work every day, spending time in the mountains, trail running and snowboarding when he can, and at least once a week takes one of the yoga classes held at the company HQ. "So I maintain this constant level of fitness," he says, "but it's not an extreme level of fitness." He just watched *Free Solo*, the film about the climber Mr Alex Honnold. "That guy trains," he says. Whereas, by contrast,

as Mr Stubbington puts it, "I've always tried to maintain a baseline – the only person I'm competing with is myself. No one's ever going to rile me up more than I rile myself up. And I've got to be thankful, because at one point in my life I was told I might not walk again. So, to me, training – be it yoga, or be it outdoors training – sometimes it's about sort of running away from myself and losing myself, and then, sometimes, it's about a more inward journey."

Indoors or out, Mr Stubbington functions as an ideal guinea pig for road-testing his designs. "At lulu," he says, "we're thinking about a guy who's on the move all the time. My friends who work in a music engineering studio or as fashion photographers or as architects, they're running from meeting to meeting or getting on a plane, and they're training. I think it's become more common for guys to be taking care of themselves now. Maybe it's an age thing, but I've always been into health and fitness, although I've always liked the other side of things, too. For me, it's about the yin and the yang. I love to be at a dive bar, but I also love going to yoga, so when you can have the two and work them into your life in a way that gels, I think there's a real beauty in that."

It is a priority for Mr Stubbington to create clothes that can go here and there, that will play at all the various speeds and in all of the various contexts through which our modern-day lives may take us. And the way that is done, Mr Stubbington says, is by designing with the function of a garment as the primary consideration. "It's almost like product design," he says, of this methodology. "We're constantly trying out new fabrics, new ways of making things to try and optimise the performance of the human, taking into account both how those clothes feel on your body, and how they feel in your mind. But we really design with this minimalist ethos that everything within the garment has to work, has to function. The function is the most important thing. So innovation comes through functionality – and that ends up creating the design."

All these designs are, of course, made for performance, but not every garment lululemon makes is ultramarathon garb. As men's lifestyles are beginning to incorporate more of a mix, so too are their offerings. "It doesn't all look like sport clothing," Mr Stubbington says, "but it has that functionality." This is the core coding that lululemon's pieces are based on. "I'm an indie kid at heart," Mr Stubbington says. "I'm not one to sit around in sweatpants, but the way we're camouflaging it is adding extra capability to clothing that you can wear every day. I love that ethos, too. I believe that guys want to feel more comfortable in their daily attire. Because you don't want to go back to something uncomfortable once you've worn something comfortable, especially when it really functions."

Mr Ben Stubbington, photographed in Vancouver by Mr Kamil Bialous

WHICH FITNESS FREAK ARE YOU?

From Cro-Magnon cardio to fingertip free soloing, whatever your exercise obsession, there's a tribe for you

Words by Mr Jamie Millar

The powerful drive to be a member of a tribe is evolutionarily hard-wired into us from an age when isolation could limit access to resources and threaten survival. Humans are social creatures. Indeed, our ability to create and maintain large groups is what separates us from the animals (along with, hopefully, our dress sense). Which explains why, to this day, we continue to strenuously seek strength in numbers – at work, at play and even in the gym.

To help you identify which fitness tribe to join, or which you're already initiated into, MR PORTER has conducted an anthropological survey of five dominant species and their distinguishing characteristics in the manner of Sir David Attenborough. *Sweat Life On Earth*, if you will. If nothing else, it helps to have moral and, occasionally, physical support, plus somebody who's interested in your regimen to talk about it with. All. The. Time.

THE PRIMAL MOVER

Yoga, callisthenics, natural movement. If a practice can be traced back thousands of years and predates the invention of Pumping Iron-age tools, then this proto-fitness hipster was into it before it became cool again after several intervening millennia. A snake-hipped part-man, part-orangutan, he eats paleo and forgoes man-made facilities in favour of Mother Earth's jungle gym, affixing his organic Olympic rings to trees, naturally occurring pull-up bars or playground equipment. Bearded and man-bunned, he squats at every opportunity to restore hip mobility as if he's having a bowel movement and wears barefoot shoes when he's not connecting sole to soil to "earth" himself.

THE BULLETPROOF MONK

Boasting more fitness trackers than limbs, this biohacking cyborg relentlessly optimises every aspect – sorry, metric – of his existence. He doesn't actually do cardio, because it oxidises the body. Not that he could fit it in between his breathing exercises, meditation and journaling, which he does while in an oxygen tent, cryotherapy chamber or flotation tank. Popping so many dietary supplements and nootropics that he rattles, he's strictly keto (fewer than 50g of carbs a day) and won't eat kale because of the arsenic, but thinks nothing of necking a pack of grass-fed butter in his toxin-free coffee. He will survive to over 100 and cannot be killed by conventional weapons, but is this living?

058

THE HAPPY BOOT CAMPER

Remarkably chipper for someone who gets up at 6.00am every morning to flagellate himself at the high-intensity boutique studio du jour, he's mainlining a seemingly inexhaustible supply of post-exercise endorphins and high fives (even if you suspect that inside, he's crying). Fitness-model handsome and buff, he shows off his impressive shape by shunning sleeved workout T-shirts and whipping his top off as soon as the warm up is over and the class hots up. Have you ever been to one, by the way? Wait, you've never been?! OMG, you should totally go! How about tomorrow? I'm booking you in right now. The instructor is amazing. He's my favourite. You're going to love it. High five!

THE OVERLY-SOCIAL CLIMBER

Lean and wiry, this spidery man can crush the bones in your hand to white powder in his calloused, blistered grip and cling to holds with a single finger but, if flipped onto his front and asked to perform 10 press-ups, will flail around helplessly like a capsized beetle. Permanently clad in outdoorsy brands such as Patagonia and The North Face even though the closest he comes to real rock is the chalk he applies to his hands at his local indoor wall, he's as quick to give you his unsolicited opinion on rope-averse daredevil Mr Alex Honnold's death-defying exploits in documentary *Free Solo* as he is "beta" info on a route – despite the fact that all he's done that day is hang around drinking coffee.

THE ULTRA COMPETITOR

Whether it's running, cycling, swimming or all of the above, this middle-aged Ironman in Lycra and a Kona finisher's tee is in it for the long haul. With a streamlined chassis that boasts a strength-to-weight ratio to rival any carbon frame, he's plant-based like his hero Mr Rich Roll and bought a Peloton with spare change found in the saddle bag of one of his astronomically priced road bikes (so he could squeeze some extra miles in either side of his pedal-powered commute, natch). Between all those hours he spends training and the high-flying job he has to hold down to afford this hobby that he coincidentally discovered after becoming a father, it's a wonder he has any time left for, well, anything else... Oh, wait.

GET MORE OUT OF YOUR EXERCISE WITH MINDFULNESS

Messrs Max Vallot and Tom Daly, creators of the athletic apparel brand District Vision, share their guide to the silent sport of mindfulness

REFLECTION

As you start your workout, find a comfortable position and close your eyes. Consider why you have chosen to commit to this activity. How did you get here? Why is this important to you? What are your objectives?

GROUNDING

Open your eyes and get a feel for your environment. Notice the light and sound. Are your feet on the ground? Rather than anticipating how all of this may affect your workout, can you be aware of it without judgement?

BODY

Begin gently. We have the best chance of building mindfulness during simple, repetitive movements. Take one body part at a time and observe how the movement affects it. What does your body feel like as a whole? If there is pain or discomfort, be mindful of it.

BREATH

The breath is always a good anchor for mindfulness, you can come back to it at any time. Try not to control it, just let it happen. As you pick up the pace, stay with it. Witness the progression inside.

EMOTIONS

When we push ourselves we tend to experience a roller coaster of thoughts and emotions. The trick with mindfulness is breaking the pattern of identifying with your mental state. Don't be a slave to your thoughts. Try not to analyse them, just let the chatter come and go.

CLOSURE

Take a few moments to cool down. Lie on the ground or sit in meditation posture. How does the body feel? What is the breath doing? Surrender all efforts. As meditation master Ajahn Sumedho says: let go, let go, let go.

EAT RIGHT FOR YOUR EXERCISE REGIMEN

Fat-burning and muscle-boosting Michelin-grade meals that are as delicious as they are nutritious

Words by Mr Mark Sansom

What you eat and drink before and after exercise is just as important as the exertion itself. We all know guys who think 45 minutes of wheezing by the five-a-side pitch as a rolling substitute, or nine holes of seriously subpar (ie, seriously over-par) pitch and putt gives them carte blanche to tuck into a burger and five beers afterwards. At the other end of the spectrum are borderline obsessives who scoff supermarket chicken breasts straight from the packet after a workout, or drink foul-tasting pond sludge all afternoon in order to get their mega-greens. Don't be either of those guys. There is a happy medium. You can eat right and still enjoy it.

We have paired the fine-dining expertise of Michelin-grade chef Mr Mark Sargeant with the nutritional nous of ex-professional rugby player and diet coach Mr Alex Ferentinos to create six healthy dishes that will help your body, whatever your fitness goal, while also tasting good. Because the two need never be mutually exclusive.

BEST FOR CARDIO NUTS

The haute-grade oatmeal

Whether you're training for a marathon or a long bike ride, or you're running the assault course of an all-day work conference, you need something to keep you going. This super bowl has all three prime components for your pre-distance breakfast: oats for slow-release carbohydrates to give your muscles plenty of fuel to burn; good-fat loaded almonds to facilitate the transfer of energy to muscles; and seeds and berries to provide a range of vitamins to aid post-exercise recovery.

Prep time
5 minutes (plus overnight soaking)
Serves 1

Ingredients
2 tbsp natural yoghurt
50ml (¼ cup) almond milk
1 scoop Bodyism Ultimate Clean
Male Optimum protein powder
1 tsp flaxseed
1 tsp chia seeds
Pinch of cinnamon
50g (½ cup) rolled oats
1 tbsp flaked almonds
Handful of blueberries

Method
Start your prep the night before. In a bowl, stir together the yoghurt, almond milk, protein powder, chia seeds and cinnamon. Mix in the oats and leave in the fridge overnight in an airtight container so that the seeds and oats expand and release their energy-giving compounds. Just before you tuck in, sprinkle with the almonds and blueberries. If you're used to breakfasting "al desko", it's far better and tastier than anything you'll get from that chain coffee shop next to your office.

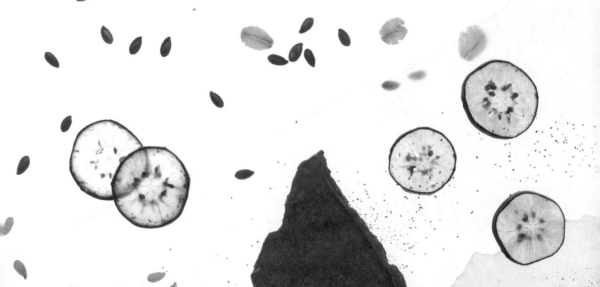

BEST FOR WEIGHT LOSS

The fat-burning curry
If you want to fire up your fat burn, ditch the salad in favour of curry.
Sounds counterintuitive, right? Studies have shown that the spices used
in Indian and Asian dishes can be great weight-loss tools. This curry is a
powerful all-rounder: it's got cinnamon to increase metabolism, cumin
to fight fat cells and turmeric to prevent the regrowth of those fat cells.

Prep time
1 hour
Serves 2 – 4

Ingredients
2 – 3 tbsp vegetable oil
1 cinnamon stick
1 clove
1 star anise
2 medium onions, diced
1 tsp ground cumin
10 cloves of garlic, crushed or grated
2 tsp Kashmiri chilli powder
½ tsp ground fenugreek
½ tsp turmeric
1 tsp salt
500g (1lb 1½oz) tomatoes, roughly
chopped
1kg (2lb 3oz) chicken thighs and
drumsticks, bone in and skinned
2 tbsp white wine vinegar
1 tsp sugar

Method
Heat the oil in a heavy-based
saucepan or a balti dish (too thin a
base means your delicate spices will
burn) and add the cinnamon, clove
and star anise. Fry for 1 minute until
they release their oils – basically,
when you can smell them. Add the
onion and fry for 10 – 15 minutes or
until softened and golden brown.

Stir in the cumin and garlic, and
fry for another 2 minutes. Next,
add the chilli powder, fenugreek,
turmeric and salt, and fry for 30
seconds. Add the tomatoes to the pan
and cook for a further 5 minutes until
they start to break down. Add the
chicken and stir everything together.
Cover the pan with a lid and cook for
45 minutes, adding a splash of water
if it starts to stick to the bottom. Stir
in the vinegar and sugar, and cook,
uncovered, for a further 5 minutes.

BEST FOR YOGA FREAKS

The super-quick superfood salad
This vegetarian dish is a well-balanced and potent combination of meat-free protein, amino acids and nutrients to help keep your muscles strong, joints supple and concentration sharp for the next time you want to nail that crow pose. Quinoa is a complete protein, meaning it contains all nine essential amino acids necessary for your body to function.

Prep time
5 mins
Serves 1

Ingredients
1 bag pre-cooked red quinoa
Juice of half a lemon
3 spring onions, sliced
5 sprigs tenderstem broccoli,
cut into chunks and blanched
Handful of kale
Half a bunch of coriander, chopped
Half a head of romaine
lettuce, shredded
Olive oil
Salt and pepper
Hot chilli sauce, such
as sriracha (optional)

Method
This one requires virtually no cooking at all, which makes it quick and easy to throw together and means you retain all the vegetables' nutrients. Just mix together all the ingredients in a bowl and season well with salt and black pepper or a little hot sauce.

BEST FOR POST-EXERCISE ACHES

The recovery burger
When recovering from contact sport or repairing muscle fibres after a hardcore weights session, harness the magic of mushrooms. Their antigen-binding lectins are like heat-seeking missiles for free radicals, the cells that cause soreness and stiffness. Turkey deals with lean muscle repair and tomatoes contain the powerful antioxidant lycopene, which is key for blood oxidation. Stacked together, this healthy burger will serve as an anti-inflammatory aid – alleviating aches and pains.

Prep time
15 minutes
Serves 1

Ingredients
2 slices turkey breast
Sea salt and freshly ground pepper
1 tsp smoked paprika
1 tbsp coconut oil
3 portobello mushrooms
4 leaves iceberg lettuce, shredded
2 gherkins, chopped
2 spring onions, sliced
1 tsp English mustard
1 tbsp mayonnaise
6 Brazil nuts, grated
2 thick slices beef tomato,
Quarter of a bunch of coriander, chopped

Method
Start by seasoning the turkey slices with sea salt, pepper and smoked paprika. Turkey is the leanest meat and should be your go-to option if you're serious about building muscle and cutting fat. Fry in the coconut oil – a healthier source of fatty acids – for about 6 minutes until cooked. Remove and keep warm. Cook the mushrooms in the same pan for 2 minutes on either side until soft and juicy. Remove and keep warm with the turkey. The mushrooms will form your burger "bun". Mix together the lettuce, gherkins, spring onions, mustard, mayonnaise, Brazil nuts and coriander, then begin to assemble in this order: mushroom, lettuce mix, tomato, turkey. Repeat until you're out of ingredients. Finish with the final mushroom and hold together with a skewer.

BEST FOR BULKING UP

The protein-packed pork loin
Eating the right stuff at the right time is key when attempting to build
muscle. Always try to eat your main meal within 30 minutes of training,
when your muscles are at their most receptive. Pork loin is a lean source
of protein that's full of flavour. The sweet potatoes' slow-release carbs
mean you don't get the insulin spike that comes with their white cousins.
(Insulin causes your body to store sugar as fat.)

Prep time
1 hour
Serves 1

Ingredients
1 medium-sized pork loin,
cut into 2in steaks
1 tbsp honey
1 tsp soy sauce
1 tbsp rice wine vinegar
1 tsp sesame seeds
1 tsp Chinese five spice,
plus extra for sprinkling
1 tbsp brown sugar
Juice of half a lime
2 bird's-eye chillies, sliced
4 cloves of garlic, sliced
Handful of bok choy
4 sprigs tenderstem broccoli
Handful of cashews
Handful of coriander, chopped
3 medium-sized sweet potatoes,
cut into chips
Olive oil

Method
Start by marinating the pork. Mix
the honey, soy sauce, vinegar, sesame
seeds, five-spice, brown sugar and
lime juice in a bowl and add the pork.
Cover with plastic wrap and allow it
to marinate in the fridge for as long
as you've got; an hour's ideal, but
15 minutes is fine.

Meanwhile, place the sweet potato
chips in a roasting tin. Drizzle with
olive oil, sprinkle on some Chinese
five-spice and mix with your hands.
Oven bake at 200°C for 20 minutes,
turning halfway.

Fry the pork and marinade for
about 8 minutes, or until the meat
is cooked through. Add the chillies,
garlic and a splash of water so it
doesn't stick. Turn the heat down and
cook for another 5 minutes.

Add a little more water, then mix
in the bok choy and broccoli. Cook
for another 5 minutes, then sprinkle
on the cashews and coriander.

HOW TO TALK TO YOUR PERSONAL TRAINER

Being honest, setting clearer
goals and other ways to maximise
your gym fitness regimen

Words by Mr Simon Usborne

Hiring a personal trainer is worth a dozen barely used gym memberships, not least if your willpower is as poorly defined as your abs. But as well as working your glutes, quads and wallet, a partnership with a PT is just as much an exercise in diplomacy, deference, confidence and honesty. You have to know what you want and how to ask for it.

"In some ways, it's quite simple – I take payment and you're on time – but outside of that, it depends on so much," says Mr Nick Finney, a leading London trainer whose clients have included Mr Robbie Williams and Ms Jennifer Lopez. "It's definitely a special relationship."

Here, Mr Finney joins a panel of experts to guide would-be clients through the pitfalls and advantages in PT partnerships. Mr Dalton Wong is the founder and director of Twenty Two Training in west London and Ms Nathalie Schyllert is CEO of Bodyism, the exclusive Notting Hill-based but global fitness club. We spoke to them all to get the lowdown.

DON'T BE AFRAID TO ASK QUESTIONS

"Before you even start, the first thing you have to do is a meet-and-greet," says Mr Wong. "What you're hiring is someone's expertise, but all trainers have that. It's the relationship you build with your trainer that's going to make the magic happen. So, I'll interview my clients and they'll interview me."

Mr Wong encourages clients to ask questions and to take a look at a PT's certificates. Good trainers will also offer references. When it can cost up to £25,000 per year to have a trainer, it's worth going the extra mile before you start. Mr Wong will also put new clients through a 90-minute preliminary assessment.

Mr Finney has initial meetings, too. "I might get vegans who want to bulk up, or steak eaters who want to lose weight. I met a new guy who has a weight problem after having cancer a year ago, but works insane hours in IT. I need to know all of this."

BE CLEAR ABOUT
YOUR GOALS, BUT
BE REALISTIC, TOO

It's good to have high expectations, but, like a sculptor, you've got to work with the material in front of you. "Don't tell me you want to look like Brad Pitt in *Fight Club*, because it's not going to happen," says Mr Wong.

There's also age to contend with. Mr Wong says: "If someone says to me, 'I want to lose 10lb, I exercise and did college sports,' I say, 'Yeah, bro, that's 15 years ago. You're not that guy anymore.'

When weight loss and shaping up is the goal (which is most of the time), Mr Wong presents new clients with two options. "I say, 'I can help you achieve your goal in six months and there's a chance it will come back, or we can do it in a year and there's a good chance it will never come back.' Some choose six months, but if you go for a year, it means we can do some really good things."

Mr Finney and Mr Wong say their clients are rarely shy, but for first-timers, it can be hard to know how much to submit or request from a trainer. "People can be scared of asking for things," says Ms Schyllert. "But every single client is different and you should make sure the trainer is working for you."

BE HONEST ABOUT
YOUR LIFESTYLE

Like hairdressers and taxi drivers, personal trainers hear a lot of things. But in their case, they need to if they are going to help you properly. "When they're physically exhausted, people tell me personal things and that's when I capture it in the memory bank so when I'm trying to encourage them later I can use it," says Mr Wong.

Clients who are reluctant to be totally honest about their lifestyles are only making life harder for themselves. "It doesn't matter if you eat 10 Mars bars for breakfast, I just need to know so we can work with it," says Mr Finney. Weigh-ins can be awkward, but Mr Finney says he is not there to judge: "I'm not looking at how much you weigh compared to me. I'm just looking for a marker."

"I'd never tell anyone off to make them feel bad," says Ms Schyllert. "And the way a trainer responds to what a client says is also going to encourage them to be more honest in the future." If your trainer makes you feel bad about yourself, look for another one.

5

DON'T DEMAND ONLY CARDIO

It's tempting to get a new pair of sneakers and just hit the streets to run. But a good trainer should be able to suggest effective ways to get fit other than aimless bouts of cardio. "We know running makes you fit, but I don't believe people should pay someone to watch them run," says Mr Finney. "My business tends to be moderating weight and just looking a bit better, you can run an hour a day and not do that. Also, the body can't cope. I've got stockbrokers coming in on two hours' sleep and they don't have the energy for it."

Mr Finney is a resistance guy. "The most effective long-term strategy for busy people is weight training," he says. With running, getting enough oxygen is the challenge. "With resistance, you can go harder, do different exercises and move faster. In two years, you're burning way more calories, but on three hours a week." And with professional guidance, you're much less likely to get an injury. Mr Finney also sets a handy goal for new clients: to be able to achieve your own weight in 10 pull-ups, press-ups, squats and deadlifts. "When you can do that, you'll look better," he says.

4

TRUST YOUR TRAINER'S ADVICE

If you've got the time and money for a personal trainer, you should find one you trust and then follow their advice. For Mr Finney, the worst thing a client can arrive with is the conflicting advice of multiple experts. "I like people who've had a trainer before because they know how things work, but it can be a nightmare when someone's already got a Pilates coach and three nutritionists and they start lecturing me," he says.

"People will say things like, 'My nutritionist says I'm not allowed eggs after midday,' or 'I can't have milk in a hot drink because it turns to bad fat.' It's utter garbage but you have to suck it up and hope they'll realise that I know what I'm talking about."

WHAT IT TAKES TO BE AS FIT AS MR LAIRD HAMILTON

Advice from the surfing god
on what to eat, drink and
do to be a tiny bit like him

Words by Mr Chris Wallace

Frankly, we could be forgiven, after all these years, for under-appreciating the sight of Mr Laird Hamilton sliding down the sheer, slippery face of one gargantuan wave after another – he makes it look so easy, even as a mountain of water threatens to swallow his 6ft 3in frame. But imagine the pure innovation required to get the Hawaii native to that point. The continuous tinkering, pushing, improving – stretching the very frontiers of fitness.

Indeed, even now, there is probably no one alive with more energy than mid-fifties Mr Hamilton, who early on in his career opted out of traditional surf competitions, finding their mano-a-mano format

unpleasant and institutional, to instead "surf as an art". Today, every morning, a motley crew of men and women – many of them giants in their particular industries – join Mr Hamilton and his wife, the legendary volleyball star and fitness guru Ms Gabby Reece, at their home in Malibu for an impromptu exercise session. Here, he gives us a glimpse of his fitness, diet and wellness regimen (as if we could ever keep up).

What's a typical day for your diet?
Hydrating well in the morning with water. I'll also drink a ginger-and-lemon water with Himalayan salt and take an ocean mineral supplement. And then I'll enjoy my coffee, which I use as a platform to work in high-quality fats, and even proteins. What I've noticed is that, the better I eat, if I get the minerals and nutrients I need, my appetite goes down – and I've been known to have a pretty insatiable appetite. Sometimes, I'll only eat one meal a day. On an ideal day, I'll have steamed or roasted veggies – cauliflower, broccoli, kale, spinach – and a good protein: either eggs or wild salmon, grilled, with avocado and a bunch of olive oil. I have people with access to wild protein, and I'll have some wild sea bass show up at my house. And then I have friends that send me boxes of vegetables from their gardens, and Gabby goes to the farmer's market.

I like a ton of variety – and growing up in Hawaii, I was exposed to a big variety of food, and I've always had a unique perspective on it. I guess, I'm keto; that's a nice way of describing it. I've been paleo since before the modern paleo revolution. I've always looked at food as fuel. I have a saying, "Potato chips in, potato chips out." If you want to perform at a high level... rockets need rocket fuel. The other night, we had a gluten-free elk lasagna that was crazy good. And then I just go off of how my body reacts. If I get some indigestion or my body doesn't respond well to something, I just don't eat that again. I got a big chaga [medicinal mushroom] pot on my stove that kind of burns 24 hours a day. I drink that at night before I sleep, and I like the way it affects my sleep and my digestion.

And variety is big in your workouts as well?
It varies all the time. I'll go do a day of yoga, and then we'll do some isometrics on another day, and then we'll do some breath work, and then we'll do lifting, or some pool work. I have some specific pool training routines that we do with weightlifting and swimming combined. I have a tendency to kind of feel it, and go with how we're feeling, modifying and adjusting things; trying to create as much variety as we can – always keeping the body guessing, adapting. I attribute part of [my adaptation] to [a fear of] boredom, to my interest in trying to continue to learn, and

Mr Laird Hamilton, photographed in Malibu by Mr Graham Walzer

having the benefits of that ever kind of learning spirit. That's where all the big gains happen.

So, I don't fully know what my work outs are going to look like. [For example,] I didn't know what I was going to do today. I was letting my body feel it. And it was intense. I had 10 men over, we heated up in the sauna and we got hot and sweaty. Then we did an isometric stance, known as a "horse", which is kind of like a sumo stance, and we were doing an evolving breathing pattern. As our fatigue level increased, we began to increase our breath in order to sustain the position, then we incorporated ice within that. One by one, after about 10 minutes of holding the stance, each guy got into this tub that was full of ice for about two minutes. Then we went back around and through it all again, working in some breath-holds too. And kind of fatigued our systems. Then we ate some charcoal, just to try help us with the detox our body went through.

I think a lot of us have lost the ability to listen to our bodies.
And our instincts have become so dulled because we don't rely on them so much anymore. A friend of mine says, "You're your own greatest doctor, at the end of the day, because no one can heal you like you can." Only you know how you're feeling, how you're responding to the medicines that you're using. And I think that's important for all of us, to start to listen to your voice that says, "I didn't get enough sleep last night, I don't feel great." Not because we're supposed to get these many hours.

Do you make special time to meditate, to get into a flow state?
I mean, that's built into everything I do. A lot of that breath work stuff, you're going to go away. You're gonna "travel".

So, if tomorrow you wake up and there is some sort of meteorological...
Phenomenon? I mean, you just drop everything. I literally open the window and look out at the ocean, and if there's surf, I'll walk right away from the training. Some of the guys will come with me, some won't. We've created these environments where we don't move, and then we're in the same routine, eating the same thing... Gabby calls it "death by domestication". On the other hand, with the way I was raised, there is a wildness in me. I'm still looking to the conditions to dictate the outcome. And it's a little bit like being a hunter – you look outside and the herd goes running by... "Hey, don't worry! I'll be back!"

How to:

DRESS FOR EXERCISE

The explosion of athleisure has left us with no shortage of options for looking great when working on our fitness. It's an embarrassment of synthetic, moisture-wicking, body-hugging riches. The challenge becomes finding the balance between visual splendour and workout gear that is actually practical. Here's how to sweat without regret.

THE GROUND RULES

It's not a fashion show

Yes, it's nice if all the elements of your gym kit aren't in wildly clashing colours (we suggest black, navy and dark green, which work together) but, whatever Instagram might imply, exercise is about performance and results, so focus on gear that will make you feel good, too.

Stock up

We are often subconsciously looking for excuses not to exercise, the lack of clean kit being one. Don't give yourself that option. Figure out how often you want to work out per week and buy that many shorts, T-shirts and socks. That way, you'll only have to wash them once a week.

Be discreet

Some people work out to let off steam. Others just want to look good in their underwear. Either way, no judgement. It's your life, but does anyone want to see naked flesh in the gym? Not really. So, wearers of low-cut, stringy vests and short shorts, perhaps save your bulging pectorals for your significant other, or *Love Island* audition, OK?

Bring a towel

The most elegant thing you can do in the gym – in any situation, really – is not to make a mess. And if you do, clean up after yourself. Today's most stylish fitness accessory, in our opinion, is a lightweight towel which, after any sort of sweat-inducing workout, you can use to wipe a) yourself and b) anything you might have come into contact with.

Treat yourself

Exercising is all about rewards, but progress tends to happen over weeks and months, which is a bit of a bore. Make it worth your while in the short term by filling your gym washbag with a curated selection of your favourite creams and potions, not just what you have lying around. Look out for useful ingredients such as peppermint, which is cooling and invigorating, and camomile, which has anti-inflammatory properties and will help tone down redness from overexertion.

THE DETAILS

The cap

Not by any means compulsory, but often left out of a workout wardrobe. Running about and doing star jumps, believe it or not, does not make you immune from the ultraviolet rays emitted by the sun. In short, don't ruin your face for the sake of your body. If you're going to be exercising outside, make sure you wear a baseball cap and, yes, lots of sun block.

The hoodie

The hoodie is helpful for exercising outside in winter and guarding against the elements walking to and from the gym. For the former purposes, look for features such as cleverly placed zip pockets, cooling vents and water-resistant fabrics. For the latter, there's only one choice (for the Rocky look, of course): a classic grey loopback cotton hoodie.

The T-shirt

Technical fabrics aren't just a gimmick. They dramatically improve the experience of both working out and cleaning up the resulting mess. Opt for sweat-wicking wool blends for your T-shirt or base layer or choose garments with quick-dry fabrics and mesh panels for extra ventilation.

The shorts

For the gym, you need to dispose of anything that you would wear to play basketball. Long and loose may be comfortable, but if you're attempting burpees, squats and the like, you need something shorter and stretchier to improve your range of motion. And all the better if the shorts come with built-in compression tights. These not only serve a therapeutic purpose but also keep, ahem, everything in the right place.

The leggings

In the time of King Louis XIV, men wore tights to show off their calves and ankles as exemplars of a good figure. Centuries later, tights are all the rage once again, but for different reasons. Sort of. Whether running or gyming, a good pair of compression tights will aid blood flow back to the heart, which helps with endurance and post-workout recovery.

3

BETTER GROOMING

HOW FIVE STYLISH MEN STAY IMPECCABLY GROOMED

Five gents on the regimens that keep them looking tip-top

Words by Mr Jamie Millar

The year is 1991. *American Psycho*, Mr Bret Easton Ellis' cult novel about Patrick Bateman, has given rise to a surprising new trend: exhaustive bathroom ablutions and borderline obsessive grooming. But, if you actually tried to follow Bateman's grooming regimen, which runs to two whole pages, you'd likely go mad – or, at the very least, miss your train.

It may be satire, but clearly something stuck. These days, men's grooming is no laughing matter. There are creams, gels, oils and waxes for every inch of our imperfect bodies, and it's only going to get worse (or better, depending on how you look at it). In the next five years, the grooming sector is set to grow into a $30bn industry. This is due, in large part, to men who are savvier than ever in their routine and choice of product, even as the marketplace explodes.

To aid in our quest for eternal beauty, we asked five of our favourite gents about their own grooming regimens. Peel-off masks optional.

MR ATIP WANANURUKS *fashion director, Highsnobiety*

The fashion director of streetwear and culture bible Highsnobiety is
suitably discerning when it comes to grooming products. "I collect and
covet scents, so the bathroom has become more like a perfumery counter,"
Mr Atip Wananuruks confesses, with TOM FORD's Noir de Noir a current
favourite. He's tried and tested most of the men's skincare lines out there
in order to find a non-chemical moisturiser that's properly absorbed by
his skin type. After showering with a lavender liquid soap, he brushes
out his "bouffant *massif*" and applies rosemary hair oil, then shapes his
beard, finishing off with a dash of Tobacco Vanille Conditioning Beard
Oil by TOM FORD. Lest you think him some kind of dallying sybarite,
Mr Wananuruks is responsible for ferrying his two-and-a-half-year-old son
to nursery every morning, so all of this is usually done within 15 minutes.

MR DOM BRIDGES *founder, Haeckels*

Dry skin and mild eczema led Mr Dom Bridges to discover the hydrating
and calming properties of seaweed, which in turn led the former adman
to launch locally-sourced grooming brand Haeckels in the previously
rundown English coastal town of Margate – now dubbed "Shoreditch-
on-Sea". Skincare-wise, he washes with Haeckels Marine Facial
Cleanser, hydrates with its Eco Marine Cream then protects with an
ocean-friendly SPF. Following a trip to Japan, he's adopted the practice
of scrubbing with a mitt in the shower, then soaking in the tub before
bed. "We consider ourselves so advanced, but we're still a bunch of dirty
Victorians compared to some of the beautiful bathing rituals in other
cultures," says Mr Bridges.

MR DAMIAN SOONG *co-founder, Form*

The founder of plant-based supplement brand Form Nutrition wakes
up early without an alarm ("one of life's great luxuries") before getting
his Peloton fix. Mr Damian Soong averages exactly seven hours and
15 minutes of beauty sleep per night, which he enhances by popping
Form Nutrition ZZZZs Supplement before turning in at 9.30pm, wearing
an eye mask and silicone ear plugs. "Sleep is the essential foundation
of everything else," says Mr Soong, who favours grooming brands that
share Form's plant-based philosophy. His skincare routine includes
moisturiser and Aesop Geranium Leaf Body Balm (which he keeps

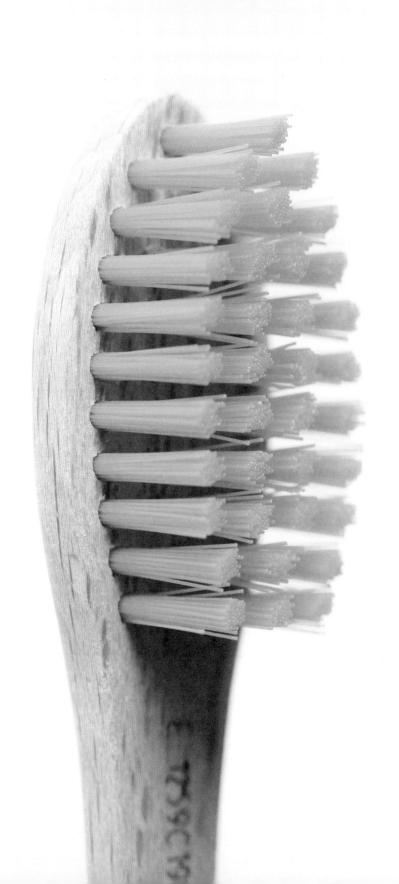

in his bathroom, office and car), collagen serum and eye cream, plus a weekly brightening vitamin C and glycolic acid mask. His hair is fine, so he employs a thickening shampoo, or a spray if he's not washing it, and cleans his teeth with charcoal paste on a plastic-free bamboo brush. He also uses Aesop Herbal Deodorant – "I was pretty shocked you could spend £23 on deodorant, but it does smell good" – while his signature scent is Byredo's Gypsy Water.

MR THOM WHIDDETT co-founder, Thom Sweeney

One half of British tailoring house Thom Sweeney, Mr Thom Whiddett looks far too young to be a 39-year-old dad of two boys who almost never lies in past 6.00am. It helps that he aims to be in bed by 10.00pm if he's not out for dinner. Mr Whiddett washes his hair with Pankhurst London Head To Toe Shampoo every morning, even though he knows that's probably too often: "But I don't feel clean – and awake – without doing so." If he's recently visited Mr Brent Pankhurst, then his barber's moulding cream is his go-to styling product; if not, he reaches for the leave-in styling conditioner. He exfoliates with TOM FORD Exfoliating Energy Scrub then moisturises with the designer's emollient ("not too thick or heavy"). Aesop Protective Lip Balm is also at the ready. Fatherly duties dictate that Mr Whiddett can only self-care so much, but he thinks it's great that men are spending more time on grooming.

MR PATRICK KIDD founder, Patricks

As the owner of an award-winning barbershop in Bondi, Australia, Mr Patrick Kidd created Patricks haircare products, which has since expanded to skincare. Unsurprisingly, what his wife calls his morning "day spa" (20 to 30 minutes in the bathroom) revolves around his own wares: SH2 Deep Clean Shampoo (formulated to help thicken hair and to remove his water-resistant M3 Matte Finish Strong Hold Pomade), CD2 Moisturizing Conditioner, AM1 Moisturizer, FW1 Face Wash and BW1 Body Wash in tandem with a "weird mesh loofah". He exfoliates with his FS1 Face Scrub (containing volcanic sand and crushed diamonds) three times a week *before* his face wash, rather than after: "It seems to keep my skin softer." A frequent flyer and dad to a "rad" toddler and newborn, he packs EB1 Triple Correction Eye Balm for excess baggage. His own brand aside, he uses La Mer Moisturizing Matte Lotion for his oily skin and, twice a week, Dr. Dennis Gross Skincare's daily micro-peel wipes.

A SPOTTER'S GUIDE TO HAIR FOR MODERN MEN

The top 15 styles to add flair to your bonce – and how to get them

Words by Ms Jessica Punter

The next time you're at your local watering hole, take a moment to examine the haircuts on display. Keen observers will note that it's a varied scene. Changing work codes and a plethora of social and cultural influences mean that the current hairstyling chart has some star performers, up and comers, re-entries and rank outsiders.

We tapped top session stylists, Messrs Lee Machin, Joshua Gibson and Davide Barbieri for their insider knowledge on the bigger grooming picture. The main takeaway? The super-sharp barber-shop look we've been so fond of is on the wane. A general relaxed approach and a series of grown-out, longer styles that focus on soft shapes and natural texture are on the rise. Read on, for the definitive guide to the modern haircuts you need to know now.

THE CAESAR

This close crop is characterised by a very high, blunt fringe or bangs. It was worn by Mr Marlon Brando in Julius Caesar, Mr George Clooney during the 1990s, Mr George Michael in the 2000s and currently by stylists and buyers on the fashion circuit.

What type of hair does it suit:
Tight curls and natural waves look more classically Roman.

What to ask for at the barbershop:
Short back and sides, high, straight fringe or bangs.

How to style it:
Use a texturising product such as Baxter of California Paste Pomade.

THE FRENCH CROP

A close cousin of the Caesar, this super-versatile cut has a soft fringe and can have a more uniform length all over, or a sharper grade and fade on the sides.

What type of hair does it suit:
Not for very fine or thinning.

What to ask for at the barbershop:
Short, blended lengths and a tidy outline.

How to style it:
Use a low-sheen wax to shape, such as Sachajuan Hair Wax.

THE MULLET

You may scoff, but ever since the third season of *Stranger Things* we've experienced a spike in all things 1980s, including the mullet of Mr Dacre Montgomery's mean alter-ego, Billy Hargrove. It's so wrong, but it won't stop its stubborn recurrence in certain hipster enclaves – see Fitzroy, Melbourne.

What type of hair does it suit:
Poker straight to wavy.

What to ask for at the barbershop:
Respectable at the front, party at the back.

How to style it:
With a light dusting of frosted highlights for the genuine period look.

THE SHAPE-UP TEMPLE FADE

As worn by the likes of Mr Anthony Joshua and Drake, this cut features a shaped fade around the temple, and a hard, straight hairline. Let the top lengths go long and natural, and you'll approach a similar style to Mr Chadwick Boseman.

What type of hair does it suit:
Dark and dense, unruly textures that need taming.

What to ask for at the barbershop:
To define and straighten the hairline, shape the temple.

How to style it:
Use a soft-bristle brush and a few drops of Sisley - Paris Precious Hair Care Oil for sheen.

THE PEAKY

A disconnected, unblended cut made incredibly popular by the Shelby mob family in the British period drama *Peaky Blinders*. You don't have to have seen the show to have the cut – it's moved far beyond its origins – check the table next to you.

What type of hair does it suit:
Fine to thick, straight to curly.

What to ask for at the barbershop:
Very short at the sides, no fade, with length left on top.

How to style it:
Comb off the face and slick with Baxter of California Soft Water Pomade, or use a little Blind Barber 60 Proof Wax and brush forwards.

THE QUIFF

The quiff is a popular fixture in men's hair and has been worn by notable men including Messrs James Dean, Harry Styles and Shawn Mendes. Go for a grown-out look for a modern feel.

What type of hair does it suit:
Most, except noticeably receding at the front.

What to ask for at the barbershop:
Scissor-cut back and sides 1 to 2in in length, square-cut top, no clippers or blunt lines.

How to style it:
Use a volumising mousse for lift and definition, blow-dry.

THE POMPADOUR

This rebellious style is never far from the pop star's repertoire. It's less oily today thanks to modern haircare formulations that switched grease for great hold. As championed by the eternally stylish Messrs Mark Ronson and David Lynch.

What type of hair does it suit:
Medium to thick, straight to wavy, a strong widow's peak.

What to ask for at the barbershop:
Short around the hairline and enough length for the 'elephant trunk' at the front.

How to style it:
With a root-lifting spray and Hanz De Fuko Gravity Paste.

THE BUZZ CUT

An easy to achieve, minimalist, military-inspired look, the buzz cut requires regular trimming to keep it looking fresh. This can be done at home or (preferably) by a barber for a precise finish.

What type of hair does it suit:
Every type, in short or great supply.

What to ask for at the barbershop:
Grade two to three all over with a gradual fade on the back and sides for a cleaner look.

How to style it:
Combine with a low, mid or high fade and lines if you feel inclined.

THE MOD BOWL

We're taking direct inspiration from recent Gucci campaigns and Mr Alessandro Michele-favoured mod-style mops that echo Brit bands, including The Charlatans' Mr Tim Burgess and early styles worn by Oasis.

What type of hair does it suit:
Fine to thick, straight to curly.

What to ask for at the barbershop:
Point cut the top so it hugs the head to encourage the ends to flick out with the fringe taking an arc line.

How to style it:
Blind Barber 40 Proof Sea Salt Spray will help achieve the bed-head look.

THE FLAT TOP

A resurgent style for black hair, the redux flat top has a softer silhouette and more moderate height than its 1990s forefather.

What type of hair does it suit:
Black hair, very tight, dense curls.

What to ask for at the barbershop:
Use clippers then freehand scissor-cut the top for structure.

How to style it:
Use a soft brush and a tiny dab of Dr Jackson's Coconut Melt 04.

THE A-LINE

It's the new "curtains" for those who recall the era-defining 1990s cut, as recently popularised by *Call Me By Your Name* star Mr Timothée Chalamet. Grungy in origin, it can be scruffy around the back with longer lengths, parted loosely on top.

What type of hair does it suit:
Mid-length, fine to thick, straight to curly.

What to ask for at the barbershop:
No clippers, soft layers around the back up to the ears.

How to style it:
Straight? Oribe Dry Texturising Spray gives a lived-in look. Curly? Use a defining cream such as Baxter of California Cream Pomade.

THE LOB (LONG BOB)

Described as the "non-haircut" look, the long bob brushes the top of the collar, with length at the front, allowing for an ear tuck. As seen on Messrs Keanu Reeves, Johnny Depp and Viggo Mortensen.

What type of hair does it suit:
Mid-weight, fine to wavy.

What to ask for at the barbershop:
Layered and point cut to keep the ends from looking blunt.

How to style it:
Blow-dry with a centre parting, use Pankhurst Defining Serum to lock down flyaway strands.

THE JAGGER SHAG

In the canon of Sir Mick Jagger hairstyles, the shag cut, inspired by his younger years, is layered around the face but longer around the back and sides (and more proportional than a mullet).

What type of hair does it suit:
Wild and wavy/curly.

What to ask for at the barbershop:
Layered from the top with length left on the bottom.

How to style it:
Apply Malin + Goetz Sage Styling Cream to damp hair, and dry naturally.

THE HIGH-FADE, HALF PONYTAIL

A style for cycle couriers, roadies, bar staff and, for a short time, Mr Colin Farrell, the high-fade, half ponytail suggests you're a free-spirited type – or possibly a European soccer player – who doesn't care what anyone else thinks.

What type of hair does it suit:
Thick and unruly, plaits and braids.

What to ask for at the barbershop:
Short to very short fade on the sides, enough length to tie up top.

How to style it:
With a zero F attitude.

THE NATURAL

Black men can always follow the lead of the original guitar hero Mr Jimi Hendrix or for a more recent example, the American quarterback Mr Colin Kaepernick, and go long with their natural texture.

What type of hair does it suit:
Very tight curls that are 2 to 3in in length.

What to ask for at the barbershop:
A taper fade at the sides, scissor-cut the ends.

How to style it:
Use a gentle long-tooth comb to tease out tangles.

HOW TO SMELL YOUR VERY BEST

Perfumer Mr Frédéric Malle on
scents and sensibilities

Words by Mr Dan Rookwood

Mr Frédéric Malle, photographed in New York by Mr Bill Gentle

Mr Frédéric Malle grew up living and breathing perfume. His grandfather, Mr Serge Heftler-Louiche, was most notably the founder of Parfums Christian Dior. His mother, as art director of the fashion house's perfumery, played a hand in the creation of Dior's legendary men's fragrance, Eau Sauvage. But Mr Malle himself began his career in 1988 at Roure Bertrand Dupont, the prestigious perfume laboratory, before founding his own fragrance house, Editions de Parfums Frédéric Malle in 2000. Here, he imparts a little of his expert knowledge to tell us how to get the most out of our scent.

Where is the best place to apply a fragrance?
I wear eau de cologne, which is not as concentrated. Therefore, I splash or spray fragrances on my chest. However, hair is probably the best spot to spray fragrance if you want to make an impression. It retains fragrance for a long time as hair is slightly oily. Also, the fragrance is permanently heated up by the head, the warmest part of your body. Having said that, be careful not to spray your hair too often as the alcohol contained in the fragrance might dry it.

Does wearing fragrance on your wrists help to diffuse the scent?
The body heat generated by pulse points such as the wrists, under the earlobes and at the base of the throat helps intensify fragrance, and can often diffuse, magnify and amplify a scent. Women often wear perfume in these places, but men can also. This is best for more concentrated fragrances, such as parfums.

Is it a good idea to rub your wrists together?
I wouldn't, especially if you apply fragrance later in the day. We generally live in cities that are quite polluted, and also our skin exudes a bit of grease. If you rub your wrists together, all that can affect the fragrance. Just let it dry by itself.

Is it true that you shouldn't spritz your face with fragrance because alcohol dries your skin?
That is true. However, many aftershaves contain emollients, which soothe and moisturise the skin. That said, I would not put cologne on my face because the higher alcohol content without emollients could dry out your skin.

Is there anywhere else you should not wear fragrance?
The part where it often smells bad is on the top of your hand. It's very strange. I think it's because of the big pores. It never smells good.

FIVE EASY WAYS TO LOOK YOUNGER

Unhappy with what you see in the mirror? Fight the signs of ageing with these expert tips to keep you youthful for longer

Words by Mr Ahmed Zambarakji

Due to our biology – thicker, oilier skin than women – many men enjoy an ageless grace period that lasts up until our thirties. But when time catches up with us, and it will, it can sometimes feel and look as though two decades' worth of damage has hit us all at once.

Much of this is due to falling testosterone levels. Without it, body fat increases while muscle mass, energy levels and, of course, libido all take a nosedive, culminating in what's been cruelly dubbed the manopause.

While there's little point trying to dodge the inevitable, there are ways of weathering the passage of time so that the journey is smoother (and more pleasant to observe). Here, we offer a few surefire solutions...

1 HAIR MANAGEMENT

By the time you reach your mid-thirties, tufts of wiry hair will begin to appear from nowhere, seemingly overnight. Earlobes sprout lengthy grizzlies, shoulders are dotted with fresh follicles and the neckline and chest hair may merge like two great rivers hell bent on cloaking your upper body in a Wolverine polo neck.

"This is likely due to long-term exposure of these follicles to hormones such as testosterone," says cosmetic surgeon Dr Benji Dhillon. In other words, marinating in hormones for 30 years has given these hairs superpowers. "Unfortunately, it does not apply to hair on the head," he says.

Lest you end up looking like a human Furby, there are effective and permanent ways of defuzzing without the need for wax strips. Laser hair removal has become increasingly affordable and you can be thoroughly deforested in just a few sessions.

Lasers target the pigment in the hair, frying the follicle until it goes out of business. "The only caveat is that hairs with little or no pigment in them (such as blonde or white hair) cannot be treated," says Dr Dhillon.

2

FINE LINES AND CROW'S FEET

Men's skin doesn't age in quite the same way as women's. "Men tend to have bigger facial muscles, which lead to more deeply etched, dynamic wrinkles around the eyes, frown area and forehead," says cosmetic dermatologist Dr Sam Bunting.

"They also have less facial fat in the cheek area, meaning there is less scaffolding to hold up the middle of the face. With age – and especially if a guy is committed to an exercise routine to keep his body in shape – the loss of this fat means men's faces can often end up looking hollow and gaunt."

The good news is that the solution doesn't have to involve a course of injectables. A high-quality vitamin C-based serum should do the trick. "They're great for brightening skin and treating fine lines, as vitamin C boosts collagen production," says Dr Bunting. "Look for a quick-drying serum that won't leave skin sticky." We recommend Perricone MD Vitamin C Ester 15 because it is a stable, high-concentration formula.

3

THE EXPANDING WAISTLINE

Even hardened gym enthusiasts will fall prey to an expanding waistline in middle age. Nutritionist Ms Rhian Stephenson of spin studio Psycle London puts it bluntly: "As testosterone declines, so does the body's ability to hold muscle mass," she says. "As a result, the body tends towards fat storage." And to add insult to injury, that excess flab is actually producing oestrogen, which lowers testosterone even further.

But restricting calories doesn't help (if anything, dieting just slows down your metabolism even more). In addition to cutting back on sugar and saturated fats, you need to choose foods that speed up your metabolism and boost testosterone levels.

"Eat plant-based wholefoods, fibre-rich foods and those naturally high in healthy, unsaturated fats to speed up the metabolism," says Ms Stephenson. "Zinc is required for testosterone production and is found in prawns, cashew nuts, poultry, eggs, quinoa, lentils and chickpeas."

Ms Elena Malmefeldt, a specialist in physiological screening, adds, "Try to include broccoli and cabbage, as they help reduce oestrogen levels."

4

AGE SPOTS

At some point in the not too distant future, skin will discolour. The hands and face of many men will become speckled with light brown spots that won't budge. Hyperpigmentation, as it is technically known, is largely due to UVA exposure over the years – a cruel reminder that you foolishly thought that an SPF 6 tanning oil qualified as adequate sunblock.

"Men are rubbish at sunscreen," says Dr Bunting. "UV exposure is responsible for at least 80 per cent of skin ageing, so this oversight has a tremendous impact." Invest in a non-sticky sunscreen that doesn't feel sticky and slap it on every day. We recommend the SPF 30 Face Moisturiser from Malin + Goetz.

As for those stubborn blemishes, Dr Bunting suggests looking into cosmeceuticals designed to target pigment and brighten the skin. "Look for ingredients such as liquorice, kojic acid and arbutin. Topical vitamin A at night, in the form of retinol, will also help." We like SkinCeuticals Advanced Pigment Corrector or Power A High Potency Vitamin A Treatment Drops from Zelens. For really stubborn spots, you'll need to see your doctor, who may prescribe some topical medication and laser treatments.

5

LAZY BONES

We like to think of bones as being "fixed", but they're living tissue and in a constant state of flux. After we hit age 30, we lose bone matter, which affects posture and joint mobility. Most guys feel this in the form of back pain, a symptom that's exacerbated by a sedentary lifestyle.

Celebrity PT Mr Dalton Wong says, "I tell clients, in your twenties and thirties, you need to focus on your front. From your forties onwards, focus on your lower and upper back as well as the glutes and hamstrings." This shift ensures a more balanced frame. "The best exercise for back health is resistance training, such as lifting weights or rowing," he says. "It increases the lean muscle mass, which makes for a stronger skeletal system that's less prone to injury."

Ms Malmefeldt implores that men "cut out the white stuff [she means sugar, wheat and white rice, BTW] and take omega-3 fatty acids to decrease stiffness." She also recommends a supplement that includes glucosamine, chondroitin and MSM, such as Solfar Extra Strength Glucosamine Chondroitin MSM, to maintain cartilage.

MR RAMDANE TOUHAMI IS REIMAGINING GROOMING

The brains behind cult Parisian grooming brand Buly 1803 shows us around his house in Tokyo

Words by Mr W David Marx

Mr Ramdane Touhami is something of a legend in international fashion circles. Throughout the 1990s, the entrepreneur pushed France's retail scene into the future with protean streetwear lines and one of the country's first concept stores, l'Épicerie, showcasing work by the likes of Messrs Marc Jacobs and Jeremy Scott. More recently, Mr Touhami has revived two of France's historical treasures: first, the candlemaker Cire Trudon, and, second, the 19th-century cosmetics brand Buly 1803. He also somehow finds time to be a DJ, writer, designer and an artist.

Growing up in a French-Moroccan family in Toulouse, Mr Touhami stumbled into fashion simply by trying to win over girls at his boarding school. "I started to do my own line of shirts at 18, when I was a skateboarder," he recalls. "There was a guy in my boarding school who was doing a line, and all the girls were in love with him. My line became much more popular than his – but I did not. Eventually I realised it wasn't the T-shirts behind his popularity. He was just very good-looking."

Mr Touhami may have lost that battle for hearts, but he won the longer war for cultural influence. That first streetwear line, Teuchy (later Teuchiland), took him to Paris, where he then started King Size – France's first true skater brand. Soon, work for other brands snowballed into a continent-hopping lifestyle. While the demand for his services saw him dragged across countries, it was his own peripatetic tendencies that led him to pull up his roots at every opportunity. "We are gypsies," he has said before of himself, his wife Ms Victoire de Taillac, and their three children. They can only bear to live in any city for a maximum of two years. "We have moved nine times in 17 years. I don't want to be stuck to a place."

At the time of writing, the timer has started to tick on his latest home, Tokyo, where Mr Touhami lives with his family in the charming Kagurazaka neighbourhood, a quiet patch of the hectic city. Their two-storey, 11-room wooden house is large by Tokyo standards, constructed in a hybrid traditional-modernist style with paper shoji doors, two separate entrances, and ample views of its Japanese garden out back. The house has a long history, originally the property of the shipbuilding family responsible for the famed WWII battleship *Yamato*.

Mr Touhami has lived around the world, but he treats a new home as a blank slate. He has spent the past few months filling the house with elegantly minimalist furniture from all over Europe. But more strikingly, he has topped the natural timber tones in each room with explosions of pop colour in lime green, royal blue and cherry-red throw cushions, low octagonal stools and curvy step seats in the corners, all of which he designed himself. The walls are covered in street art and giant film posters of cult films such as *Kids* and *Raging Bull*. His bedroom spaces

Mr Ramdane Touhami, photographed in Tokyo by Ms Daisuke Hamada

remain Japanese, however, with Mr Touhami and his wife sleeping on futons on tatami mats.

Mr Touhami has a long history with Japan, first coming in 1996, following a chance meeting with a Japanese tourist in Paris, who casually told him he should visit. Mr Touhami departed for Tokyo that very day. "I asked, 'Can I crash at your place?' And he didn't really understand what I was saying. I ended up arriving at Narita Airport before he did. He had to hide me in his garage and didn't tell his family. The parents were very old people and shocked when they found me." A year later, Mr Touhami made a better-planned return visit to help a French denim brand open a new store. But things went equally haywire. "At a dinner, I was talking to someone who said he came in a Ferrari. And I thought he must be kidding. I said, 'Let's do a bet. If there is a Ferrari in the parking lot, I get to drive it.' We went out, and it was a 1970s Ferrari. But it was an automatic, which I had never driven before. And guess what happened? I crashed the Ferrari."

Unsurprisingly, he never hit it off with the Ferrari owner, but kept coming back to Japan five to eight times a year on other assignments. In 1999, he moved to Tokyo for two years to remodel the popular retail chain And A. Now he has again chosen the city to act as his base for global operations. Contrary to Tokyo's reputation as our *Blade Runner* future, the appeal has nothing to do with speed and technology. "Tokyo doesn't change," says Mr Touhami. "It's crazy how it doesn't change. I love the *calm* of the biggest city in the world." His children go to school on the city's last tram line.

Perhaps this calm is necessary for Mr Touhami's intensive work for Buly 1803. The polymath made his first step into cosmetics in 2002 with the opening of the Parfumerie Générale in Paris. There he became obsessed with providing customers with an endless variety of products. "We had 145 brands, which was absurd in this business," he says. He brings the same approach to Buly 1803 – taking a store established in 1803 on Rue Saint-Honoré in Paris that only made fragrance, and turning it into a 21st-century global brand selling 700 items.

Mr Touhami says he loved having to create within the "frame" of a historic brand. "We had a template," he explains. "We have to create a 19th-century brand as if we're in the 19th century." That meant limiting packaging to materials from the era (no plastic), but also paying tribute to past cultural standards. His men's goods, for example, are made for an age when gentlemen were gentlemen. "In the 19th century, there was no 'men's grooming' other than shaving and toothpaste," he says. Being conscious of the brand's heritage, however, has not stopped Mr Touhami from inventing completely new categories of products – most notably his water-based perfumes in 12 different scents.

Buly 1803's combs also reveal how Mr Touhami has discovered novelty through tradition. Using acetate from Italy's premier manufacturer Mazzucchelli, Buly 1803 produces them at Europe's last true comb factory in Switzerland. Unimpressed with the limited selection of present-day styles, Mr Touhami pushed the factory into full-scale revival. "I asked them to show me what they made in the 1950s, because they seemed to only make five kinds of combs right now," he says. "They said, 'We used to make all these kinds of combs,' so I said, 'Let's make all of them!' A very stupid idea, but I am pretty proud that we have the largest selection of combs in the world. I don't want these kind of things to disappear."

Preservation of lost culture is Buly 1803's most crucial mission. Mr Touhami proudly sells *minebari* wooden women's combs made at the same shrine in the Kiso region of Japan that makes them for the Emperor. The production process takes an absurdly long time: 300 years for the *minebari* trees to grow, 100 years for the wood to dry, and then three years for the artisans to carve the combs and bathe the wood in camellia oil.

While Mr Touhami has found this particular treasure in Japan, he is always jetting off to discover other forgotten "beauty secrets", personally meeting the farmers around the world who provide the raw materials for Buly 1803's oils and clays. No part of the process is easy. The water for the brand's toothpaste comes from a single well in southwestern France, famous since Roman times for its miraculous powers of dental hygiene.

A lifetime of work in the fashion industry may inform Mr Touhami's obsession with detail, but Japan has pushed this mania into overdrive. He looks to the Japanese ideal of *honmono* – the idea that there are "authentic things" that tower in quality over the cheap, mass-produced items from most modern companies. Mr Touhami also takes lessons from the "customer is God" school of shopping culture in Japan. "You always think you are the best, but then you go to Japanese shops and, in terms of service, the way they display things, you're like, 'Oh, we have so many things to do!'"

Despite having spent so much time in Japan over the years, Mr Touhami is far from being bored. "I know Shibuya, Shinjuku, Harajuku, Nakameguro, Daikanyama and Ginza by heart," he says. "I have done them so many times. But there is no limit to discovery in Tokyo. You think you know something? You know nada." And living in northern Tokyo means it's fast to get out of the city for exploration of the countryside. At the weekend, the family heads out to the mountains near Minakami Onsen or the beaches in Zushi. On a normal day, however, Mr Touhami finds pleasure in the basic Japanese lifestyle. The first thing he does upon returning to Japan from his travels abroad? "I eat 300 yen soba [buckwheat noodles]. And then I go to work."

How to:

STOCK YOUR BATHROOM CABINET

The days when a man's grooming regimen consisted of a splash of aftershave and a defiant attitude are long behind us. Now the whole affair is a lot more complex, with a huge range of male-focused skin and haircare products on the market. In fact, there seem to be more and more of them each year, which can be confusing. However, armed with the right knowledge, it's very possible to steer one's way through it all elegantly. Here's how to find the right products and the right practices, and so, perfect your morning ablutions.

THE GROUND RULES

Declutter

You are almost certain to have some products in your cabinet that, in all honesty, you don't use. Bin ancient fragrances (they do go off, you know), festive gift sets and anything empty (even if there are two drops left). If you haven't used it in a month, you probably won't – why keep it to tumble off the shelf while you search for the thing you actually need?

Know your skin type

There is no one-size-fits-all approach to skincare. Work out if you have oily skin (prone to breakouts and shininess), dry skin (prone to redness and irritation) or combination skin (prone to all of the above), and find products that address your specific concerns. Do your research and see our grooming glossary (p. 111) to identify the key terms you need to know.

Apply the right amount

It's wasteful to use more of a product than you need, and pointless to not use enough. Which is why you should always follow the instructions precisely. And while rubbing hair gels and pastes between your hands first is helpful for creating an even finish, the same logic doesn't apply for moisturisers and serums – they should be applied directly.

Control the temperature

You wash your hands with hot water, but a more nuanced approach is needed for facial skincare purposes, as very hot water can cause dryness and irritation. Steam, on the other hand, opens pores for deeper cleansing. We recommend steaming in the shower, then cleansing with cold water – it has the effect of tightening up pores for a smoother finish.

Look to the sun

The sun's UV rays are a – if not, *the* – main cause of skin damage. Thankfully, many moisturisers now come with SPF protection, and there are even products, such as Dr. Barbara Sturm's Sun Drops, that can be used to add it to those that don't. Either way, whether it's a blazing hot day or merely overcast, make sure you've got yourself covered.

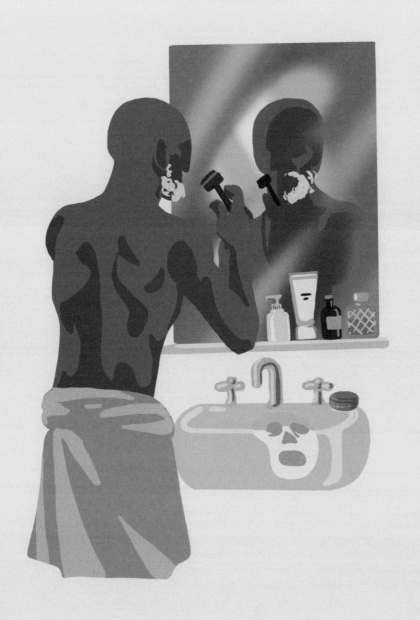

THE DETAILS

The cleanser

We don't need to tell you to wash your face, do we? Let's hope not, but we might need to remind you that your cleanser should be calibrated to your skin type. Oily skin? Opt for something geared towards acne with powerful active ingredients. Dry and combination skin? Look for the word "gentle" on the bottle. Before shaving, try an exfoliating cleaner or scrub.

The razor

There is an awful lot of nonsense around razors, modern variations of which come in various ridiculous varieties. We like the old-fashioned, safety razor type, not only more sympathetic to the feng shui of your bathroom, but also to the environment. Follow up with a post-shave treatment with exfoliating and soothing ingredients to avoid blemishes.

The serum

It sounds like something Indiana Jones might go in search of. But in the real world, serums are viscous liquids that tend to be packed with a potent concentration of active ingredients to treat specific concerns (hyaluronic acid for wrinkles, vitamin C for dull skin, etc). They should go on after your wash and shave, and before your moisturiser.

The moisturiser

The star product of your grooming regimen. A moisture-enhancing product, yes, but also a barrier that will protect your skin. Oily-skinned people should look for "oil free" products, while dry-skinned folk can handle something richer. For combination skin, opt for a "mattifying" or gel moisturiser, but try out a few to see what suits you best.

The eye cream

The skin under your eyes is the thinnest on your face, and thus most damage-prone. It's here that the first signs of ageing tend to show. Slow them down considerably with an eye cream – a light moisturiser packed with anti-inflammatory ingredients that will keep your peepers looking fresh. Apply along the bone of your eye socket, not on the lid itself.

4

SMARTER WORKING

SIX OF
THE WORLD'S
MOST STYLISH
OFFICES

The workplaces where design
is as important as business

Words by Mr Jonathan Openshaw

CASSINA *Meda, Italy*

Located in the furniture manufacturing heartland of Brianza in
Northern Italy, the 1940s headquarters of design brand Cassina
is a classic example of the *casa bottega* (home workshop). Historically,
the compound provided living spaces for the Cassina family as well as
design and production studios. Some long-standing employees remember
Mr Umberto Cassina's wife hanging out the washing in the main stairwell.
For its 90th anniversary in 2017, the brand's polymath art director
Ms Patricia Urquiola wanted to harness this history while updating it for
a 21st-century business. As you'd expect from a designer of her standing,
the details are impeccable, with Le Corbusier sofas, Mr Piero Lissoni
tables and even a recreation of a futuristic, cylindrical recreation space
designed by Ms Charlotte Perriand and Mr Pierre Jeanneret in 1938.

GUCCI *Milan, Italy*

The renovation of this Caproni aeroplane factory was a labour of love for Italian architecture practice Piuarch, even before Gucci climbed on board. "Caproni did not just build aeroplanes here," says Mr Francesco Fresa, founding partner of Piuarch. "He created a small city." This restoration of tree-lined squares, communal gardens and hangar-like workspaces caught Gucci's eye, and now the old plant has become a multifunctional headquarters for the luxury brand, which combines exhibition space with showrooms, recreation areas and offices. Just as Mr Giovanni Caproni laid down a blueprint in 1915 for his vision of a modern working community, the new Gucci offices blend work, culture and leisure in one urban complex. The vaulted aircraft hangars now host runway shows and conferences, while the shed-style roof connects the indoor and outdoor space and floods the interiors with natural light.

TOM DIXON *London, UK*

British designer Tom Dixon became the latest brand to move into the buzzing King's Cross Granary Square redevelopment in 2018, joining Google, LVMH and Central Saint Martins in the area. "It was time to try something new," says Mr Tom Dixon, who had been based in Ladbroke Grove in west London. "I see the building as being the beginning of an adventure rather than a fait accompli. I see it evolving very quickly. I want to open it up even more, to open up our design, prototyping and interiors processes." As a step towards this, alongside offices, the space has a shop, restaurant and workshop. The latter is key because it means Mr Dixon can start manufacturing in the heart of London again, something the brand has not been able to do since its early days. This integrated approach shows that new office spaces can be transformative for a brand and business, as well as the day-to-day operations of a company.

VITSŒ *Royal Leamington Spa, UK*

The British furniture manufacturer Vitsœ has always set its stock against rampant consumerism. Founded in 1959, the company operates

Previous page: Cassina, Meda. *Opposite page, from top*: Gucci, Milan; Tom Dixon, London; Vitsœ, Royal Leamington Spa

125

Above: AmorePacific, Seoul. *Below*: Powerhouse Brattørkaia, Trondheim

with a motto of "living better with less", and famously shut up shop on Black Friday to protest against what it called the "insanity" of discount culture. It's only fitting, then, that its headquarters in Royal Leamington Spa in Warwickshire, which opened in 2017, is a restrained space of beechwood, light and air. "Natural materials, natural lighting and natural ventilation were critical to restore a connection between the building's users and the world around them," says managing director Mr Mark Adams. The building is a statement of intent.

AMOREPACIFIC *Seoul, South Korea*

The appeal of South Korean beauty titan AmorePacific's innovative headquarters extends far beyond the superficial. The beautiful and holistic building is distinguished by vast "hanging garden" voids that integrate the structure with its surroundings, and a smart, sustainable facade, composed of elliptical aluminium strips. Devised by David Chipperfield Architects, the almost-square edifice offers the company first-class functionality within an environment primed to enhance staff wellbeing via the likes of roof gardens, health and fitness facilities and airy social spaces, including an elevated courtyard. Simultaneously, the wholly open atrium – which doubles as a gallery space, concert venue and lecture hall – entices the wider community to enjoy further public amenities such as a museum, daycare centre, tea room and library.

POWERHOUSE BRATTØRKAIA *Trondheim, Norway*

The northerly Norwegian city of Trondheim may not be the most obvious place to build a solar-powered office, seeing as it receives just five hours of sunlight a day during the winter. All the more remarkable then that Oslo-based architects Snøhetta unveiled the Powerhouse Brattørkaia in 2019: a building that not only covers its own energy needs but acts as a mini power station for the city blocks around it. This architectural alchemy is achieved through a roof covered with almost 3,000m2 of solar panels, carefully positioned at a 90-degree tilt to the southernly sun. Alongside innovative insulation, this allows the building to harvest twice as much energy as it takes to run across its lifetime – including construction and eventual demolition – meaning it can give a little back to its neighbours. With sustainability climbing the agenda for any self-respecting business, could Powerhouse Brattørkaia light the way for the offices of the future?

CAREER ADVICE FROM OFF-WHITE'S MR VIRGIL ABLOH

The boundary-pushing designer reveals his working habits

Words by Mr Adam Welch

It's well-documented that Mr Virgil Abloh has workaholic tendencies. Until his doctor simply insisted that he take a lengthy time out last autumn, the designer was subsisting on four hours of sleep per night and taking over 300 flights per year – the flesh and blood epitome of the new mood in fashion: fast, multi-channel, always on.

It's no surprise that Mr Abloh is a busy man. As well as helming Off-White – the streetwear-meets-luxury brand he launched in 2013 – he's also been serving as artistic director of menswear for Louis Vuitton since March 2018. And then there are the other projects. In 2018, he had: Off-White x Jimmy Choo; Sunglass Hut; Chrome Hearts; Timberland. In 2019, there came the wildly successful Off-White x Nike; Virgil Abloh x Ikea, Evian and Vitra. As the uber creative admits – he seldom says "no".

"Modern Office", 2019's capsule collection for MR PORTER, was inspired by a workplace that Mr Abloh, a former architect, once imagined he might end up occupying. But this wasn't the first time he'd seen clothing as a lens through which to contemplate professional life; his AW18 collection had the subtitle "Business Casual". Clearly, "work" is always on Mr Abloh's mind. So we picked his brains for advice, tips and career hacks.

Mr Virgil Abloh, photographed in Milan by Mr Alessandro Furchino Capria

DON'T CALL IT WORK

Mr Abloh refers to himself as many different things, often not simply a "designer". Last summer, he referred to himself as an "assistant" to *Hypebeast* magazine, to explain the fact that he feels his work is merely extending a lineage of artistic innovation in the tradition of Mr Andy Warhol and Mr Jean-Michel Basquiat. What's clear about what he does, though, whatever he calls it, is that he makes work his life and his life his work. That, he says, is the only way he can manage the hectic schedule.

You're clearly a driven person. Where do you think it all comes from?
I think it's in my DNA, it's in the way I was raised. I've always followed my passion. And if you follow your passion, your passion becomes your occupation, then you never work a day in your life. When I was working as an architect, I was also working in music, designing album covers for friends. I never think of things as one thing or the other. It's like "do both". And that's how I ended up where I am now. I believe in multitasking at core.

WORK HARD, BUT TAKE SHORTCUTS

In Mr Abloh's 2017 presentation to the Harvard University Graduate School of Design, he included some slides in red, asking crucial questions and directives that, in his opinion, every designer should consider (eg, "What's Your Signature?", "Personal Design Language"). He called these "cheat codes", things you can do to get on in life that little bit quicker.

Should you always be looking for shortcuts?
For sure. A shortcut only happens by chance, you can't bank on it. But that's sort of how life works. There are shortcuts for everyone. I believe that coincidence is key, but coincidence is energies coming towards each other. You have to be moving to meet it. There's a natural coincidence of life. But I think that when you work hard, things naturally advance. Of course, it becomes a traffic jam at points, but that's when I operate at my best. Under the pressure to complete, or to come up with a narrative.

MAKE EVERYWHERE YOUR OFFICE

Mr Abloh is always on the move. For the most part, that means he's available solely on WhatsApp. According to the man himself, he has a separate WhatsApp chat group open for every different project he's currently working on. At the time of this interview, that was about 30.

You're famously always on your phone. Why is the smartphone such a great working tool?
Well, because it's built to multitask. It removes you from being plugged in to a corporate desk-like place. All of a sudden, everywhere is an office. If I have a fully charged phone, I can do anything.

EMBRACE CHAOS

Of course, the flipside of being available anywhere, any time, is that you're available anywhere, anytime. As we speak, he's delivering instructions to assistants and beavering away on his phone in the background.

A lot of the rhetoric around phones is that they're a distraction. Do you welcome distractions?
For me, in a way, yes. Sometimes, when I'm distracted is when I think of a good idea. So, you can't always call it a distraction. It's the chaos of life.

Does anything about work make you anxious?
Almost everything. I might be driven by anxiety. As a creative, you're always fighting against not having any ideas. That might be the driver.

WORK WITH THE RIGHT PEOPLE

Mr Abloh's career history is one of collaboration. It was his partnership with Mr West and his work on the rapper's *Watch The Throne* album in the early 2010s that made him a household name. Since then, he's teamed up with Messrs Heron Preston, Matthew Williams and more to form the fashion collective Been Trill and sought meetings with other heroes and mentors, including graphic designer Mr Peter Saville. For Mr Abloh, it's not just about what you do, but whom you do it with.

What do you look for in the people you work with?
For starters, someone who I identify with, someone who I think is authentic. "Two heads are better than one," is something I firmly believe in. Collaboration is what happens with everyone in my offices and I believe in extending that outwards. I look for someone who has an authentic voice so that, together, we can make something that we couldn't individually.

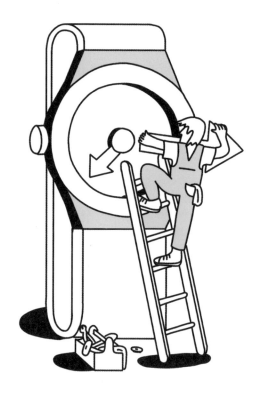

HOW TO IMPROVE YOUR TIME MANAGEMENT

Don't work harder, work smarter – these five tricks will revolutionise your daily grind

Words by Mr Oliver Burkeman

You are, as you may just possibly have noticed, too busy. That's been the universal modern complaint since at least 1910, when the English journalist Mr Arnold Bennett wrote a self-help book entitled *How To Live On 24 Hours A Day*. (It's a little enraging to read it in 2020, since it's clear that Mr Bennett's intended audience are ordinary, time-pressed professionals... with servants. Servants!) But recent years have brought an additional, painful realisation: most of the time-management methods preached by business gurus and motivational speakers – instructions, supposedly, for getting out of this mess – don't make things better. They actually make matters worse.

The problem is that we've come to think of ourselves as being like machines, or computers. If you want more output from one of those, you either make it more efficient or run it for more hours. But neither tactic works on human brains.

There is a better way. But it involves rethinking what "time management" means: not a mad dash to hyper-efficiency (which won't work and would be no fun if it did), but a savvier approach to deciding what's worth doing to begin with, and using your limited energies wisely. You'll never "get everything done" – there's an infinite number of things you could do, yet the same number of hours per day as in 1910. And if you don't decide how your hours get used, someone else will.

HARNESS THE POWER OF MOMENTUM

The first hour of the morning has been called "the rudder of the day" – how you spend it seems to set the tone for the rest. (Mr Marcel Proust took a leisurely breakfast of croissants and opium; Mr Benjamin Franklin sprang out of bed to start making plans.) Dedicate the first hour of the working day to projects that require deep focus, rather than checking email, and something remarkable happens: distractions will be less likely to carry you off once you do visit your inbox. Start scattered, in contrast, and you'll probably stay scattered until dinner.

USE THE 4.30PM
EMAIL TRICK

Mr Tom Stafford, a cognitive
scientist, passes on the following
sneaky email tactic: hold off sending
emails until 4.30pm, and you'll
minimise the chances of anyone
replying the same day. This is no
mere work-avoidance strategy for
the lazy. It also lets you benefit from
"batching", which refers to the fact
that it's easier to get more done when
you group tasks by type, instead of
switching between different kinds.
The more you can nudge people into
emailing you back the next morning,
the easier it'll be to pick a time
in advance – 11.00am to midday,
say – then plough through all your
messages at once.

CREATE TIME ASSETS,
NOT TIME DEBTS

Some tasks are equivalent to
investing money in stocks or a
savings account – by spending time
on them now, you'll create more time
later on. (Examples include taking
time to hire the right people so you
can happily leave them to do their
jobs; or building an app that keeps
selling once you've moved on to other
things.) Other tasks are more like
spending cash on a car that keeps
breaking down: you're just creating
time sucks for the future. (Example:
taking on tedious new duties because
you don't dare say no.) Some time
debts are unavoidable. But when
assessing new tasks, it's worth
asking: will this pay time dividends
later, or leave me footing the bill?

4 STRUCTURE YOUR DOWNTIME

In the midst of a grinding working day, it's tempting to imagine that, once leisure time arrives, you'll want to be sprawled on the sofa dozing, watching TV or staring addle-brained at the internet. You won't, though. Research suggests that we enjoy unstructured time off much less than we think – and find work more satisfying than we expect, because it provides regular opportunities to meet goals and feel a sense of progress. So not only is it more constructive to make social plans, adopt new hobbies or sign up for classes, it's more restorative, too. Plus, you'll be less tempted to let work seep into leisure time by checking your email.

5 EMBRACE THE KITCHEN TIMER

Your friends will look at you strangely – certainly if personal experience is anything to go by – but there are few tricks quite as effective as carrying a kitchen timer wherever you go. (Self-conscious? You have permission to use the timer on your smartphone.) Set it for 90-minute work sprints, followed by 30-minute breaks: according to the performance coach Mr Tony Schwartz, that's the optimum rest/work balance. Or power through procrastination by setting it for five minutes; even the most intimidating or arduous tasks are bearable for that long. You may be surprised to find, once the buzzer goes off, that you don't want to stop after all. Either that or your servant will come running.

PROFESSIONALESE: THE ESSENTIAL VOCABULARY

If you don't have the bandwidth to own any new action items, relax. MR PORTER's guide to office lingo is here to help

Words by Mr Adam Welch

Ah, work. Everyone has to do it. Or, you know, turn up once in a while and make some sort of affirmative noise over the top of the cappuccino foam. It's preferable that these soundbites should be intelligible (but not entirely necessary). The main thing is that something is said. Anything, really. Judging by the fury and desperation with which the office-bound spit out those fiery syllables, this is critically important. It's almost as if, without the arbitrary opening of mouths, lazy loosening of vocal chords and free flapping of lips in air-conditioned boardrooms, the glorious cathedral of capitalism would instantly collapse into silent, frowny ruins. Given the consensus is that extracting financial compensation from your employer requires you to speak – what exactly should you say? MR PORTER has compiled a complete "drill-down" (vague catch-all implying depth) on "freeballing" (speaking) in professionalese, arranging our "findings" (baseless assumptions) by key work scenarios, and fully translating each phrase to reveal what it really means.

THE KICKOFF

The process of flailing around to figure out what you're supposed to be doing.

The first thing you might find yourself doing at work is coming up with some sort of task to complete. Many professional types find that introducing such activities into the working day really helps to fill out those hours between nine and five when you aren't going for coffee, drinking coffee, or staring at your empty coffee cup. And for the task to seem worthwhile, you will also need a "mission statement" (inspiring yet ethereal slogan), possibly related to "core values" (one or more SEO keywords) or "DNA" (the most obvious and predictable aspect of whatever your company/brand/client stands for). The following phrases should come in handy at this stage.

The vocab

"What we really need to focus on here is innovation."
Unfortunately, someone is going to have to come up with an idea.

"We need to shift the paradigm of this business model."
Let's just ignore all the research and do something hasty and showy, with lots of Venn diagrams.

"Let's first get all our ducks in a row."
Shall we just faff around for a bit?

"Are we ignoring the low-hanging fruit here?"
Let's just do whatever we did last month. Does anyone know how to use the photocopier?

"Let's peel the onion."
This is a complete mess – shall we try and do something about it? PS, I'm going to cry.

"This is all about engaging millennials."
Can someone please update Instagram?

THE BRAINSTORM

A sort of tombola of interchangeable ideas. Like Boggle, but with people instead of dice. And, crucially, not fun.

It's a long-standing tradition among speakers of professionalese that the best way to get from the "what" to the "how" is to force 17 people to sit in a room and shout at each other until everyone gets bored and tired and gives up. In such situations, when nature is allowed to take its course, the group settles on an idea proposed by the loudest and most fluent professionalese speaker. If you have the requisite stamina, posture and volume, and are interested in making sure your idea is the one that makes it through, season the conversation with one or two of the following gems.

The vocab

"Why not let the data decide?"
Your idea stinks.

"We should stick to best practice here."
Stop disagreeing with me.

"Yeah, I can wear that hat for a moment."
I'm going to pretend to listen to you, but secretly I'm playing *Tetris* in my head.

"Can I just talk to that for a second?"
This is my show, shut up.

"Wow, there's some great thinking here."
Whatever we do, let's ignore whatever this mess is.

ACTIONS

Ostensibly, what you get paid for doing. Don't worry, it's mostly just sending emails.

Once you've got a mission statement and an idea, then it's time to start the real work, which is often referred to as "actions" or "action points", ie, "googling things"). Actions can only be completed if you give "110 per cent" (talk loudly about what you're doing rather than actually do it). Unless, that is, that everything is happening "organically" (where everyone waits around hoping the desired result will just materialise by itself). In both situations, you unfortunately only have two professional-ese pronouns with which to organise all this. It's a subtle distinction, and you'll have to use your own judgment to decide whether you need to say "we" (usually best for insinuating/ demanding) or "you" (which is more useful for incriminating/ blaming/outsourcing). Sample usage is outlined above, right.

The vocab

"What we need to do is…"
Someone else can deal with the details and I'll take the glory. Thank you.

"Can we just change the…"
Do as I say. Do it.

"Did you manage to…"
It's abundantly clear you've been twiddling your thumbs for a week now – time for a smackdown!

"Do you have bandwidth?"
I need to fob this off on to someone else – you'll do.

AT WORK WITH MR GILDAS LOAËC

MR PORTER steps into the stylish office of the man behind Maison Kitsuné

Words by Mr Chris Elvidge

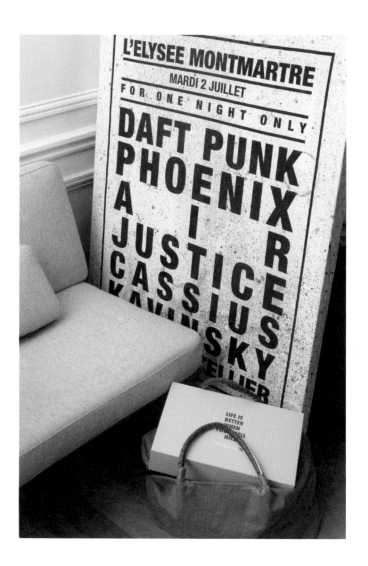

I t's a hot and sticky afternoon in Paris. Up on the fourth floor of number 10, Rue Chauchat, the windows of Mr Gildas Loaëc's office have been thrown wide open to let the air in. Down on the street below, passers-by are being treated to the synth-driven sound of Parcels, an Australian five-piece outfit, signed to Mr Loaëc's music-meets-fashion label, Kitsuné.

"They're designed for a club," he says – straining to make his voice heard over the metre-high, twin JBL speaker-cabinets that are currently causing his office walls to shake and pedestrians several storeys below to glance up in confusion – "around 200, 250 capacity." It's not entirely clear what the JBL speakers are doing in a room that would struggle to accommodate half a dozen people (let alone 250), but you sense it would be pedantic to ask.

The brainchild of Mr Loaëc and his creative partner Mr Masaya Kuroki, Kitsuné launched in 2002 as a record label specialising in hip electro compilations, before branching out into clothes, under the banner Maison Kitsuné (a coming together of the French for "house" and the Japanese for "fox"). As the co-founder and artistic director of the brand, Mr Loaëc is responsible for the music side of the business, while Mr Kuroki, who is based in Tokyo, heads up the Maison Kitsuné design studio. "We liked the idea of creating a brand that reflects the things we're passionate about," he explains of the multidisciplinary nature of the business. "We like to think of Kitsuné as a mirror into our lives."

Mr Loaëc got his start in the music industry early. Having moved to Paris from western France at the age of 19, he was soon managing a record store. It was there that he met Messrs Guy-Manuel de Homem-Christo and Thomas Bangalter, soon to become known as the helmet-clad robotic DJ duo Daft Punk. "They were customers of mine. We became friends, and I started living with Gold Helmet," he says, referring to Mr de Homem-Christo.

He couldn't have timed it better: the outfit was just about to release their breakout hit, 1995's "Da Funk". As part of a tight-knit inner circle, Mr Loaëc became responsible for a number of management and artistic roles within the band. He continued to work closely with them for the next 15 years – during which time they became one of the world's biggest DJ acts.

Reminders of that time can be spotted throughout the office: sew-on Daft Punk badges on the shelves, album artwork stacked up against the wall, a gold plaque for Daft Punk's 2001 record *Discovery* on the mantelpiece and, perhaps most notably, sitting in the fireplace, a framed photograph of Messrs Loaëc, Bangalter and de Homem-Christo in front of the Eiffel Tower, taken when they were all still in their early twenties. "Daft Punk, unmasked," he smiles.

You spent most of your twenties and thirties on tour with one of the biggest bands in the world. How have you adjusted to life behind a desk?
I appreciate how lucky I was to see the world with them. We were so young! And that experience provided me with a huge amount of inspiration when we created Kitsuné. But I still see them now – they were in the office a few days ago, sat right over there [points to the sofa].

How long have you been in this office?
About three years now. I don't know how many offices we've been through, but we're currently looking to expand again. We already have two floors in this building, and there's some space upstairs that we can take.

How many people do you have working for you?
About 50 people here, and if you include the showroom and the Paris retail stores it's around 70 in total. We've got another office in Tokyo, where we're around 25 – so overall that's nearly 100.

You've got some interesting pieces of art in this space.
Yeah, but the only really collectable stuff was given to me by friends. The Mickey Mouse figurines are by Kaws, who we've collaborated with before. They're one-of-a-kind: they're supposed to have been melted by a nuclear blast. And the Dream Concert Poster, featuring Daft Punk, Air and Phoenix, was given to me by André. He's another friend. A real art collection is still outside of my budget.

What made you choose the 9th arrondissement?
Well, it's very central, so it's super convenient in terms of getting around. One of our main stores is 200m down from here, and our showroom is nearby, too. I live a five-minute walk away.

The staff here are very chic. Do you encourage them to dress head-to-toe in Maison Kitsuné?
Of course, there are certain benefits to working here! But the wonderful thing about our staff is that they're already passionate about the brand. We don't have to encourage them too much.

Music, fashion, café culture – do you ever worry that you're diluting the brand?
No, because Kitsuné has always been a multifaceted venture. It was created as something that people could engage with in different ways, that appeals to people of all ages, and that can work in Tokyo, London or Paris. Vitally, we only do things that we're passionate about.

Mr Gildas Loaëc, photographed in Paris by Mr Jean-François Gaté

WHY SUCCESS ISN'T EVERYTHING

Or indeed, anything, really.
So why are we so obsessed with it?

Words by Mr Adam Welch

O ne of the most successful stories we've ever published on MR PORTER – depending on how you judge success – was about success itself. The headline, "Five Habits Of Successful (And Famous) Men", is, let's face it, borderline clickbait, if not the very definition of the term. But that's beside the point. The point is: wouldn't you click it? Or at least be tempted?

As I have learnt in the course of editing dozens of such pieces, the truth is that "success" is one of those words that has cut-through. And, says Mr Jamie Millar, a fashion and fitness writer whom I often commission on this topic (and the man who gave us "Five Habits Of Successful (And Famous) Men"), the idea of success has become "more compelling, or urgent, in the modern neoliberal era". "We're all at the mercy of the market and the weight of individual responsibility is crushing," he says. "You can be anything you want – but you have to do it without job security, workers' rights and other safety nets. So although these narratives are couched in terms of 'success', the subtext is 'not failing'... [not] falling by the wayside."

Mr Millar is right. Success is everywhere, and we are conditioned to want it, chase it, measure it. Data, which quantifies success day-by-day, hour-by-hour, suffuses not just the workplace but also the personal sphere – thank you social media platforms. Indeed, our love of data has given us a new language of success. After all, what is really meant by "reach", "engagement", "dwell time", "likes", "comment rate", if not "success", "success", "success?" and "SUCCESS!!!?" Meanwhile, the more metrics we have, the more confusing the issue becomes. The nagging question persists: if success is all of these things, then what, exactly, is it?

Let's turn to some experts: "Success in life could be defined as the continued expansion of happiness and the progressive realisation of worthy goals." (That's Mr Deepak Chopra in his 1994 book *The Seven Spiritual Laws Of Success*.) "The real mantra of success is sustainability and growth." (That's Mr Steven Covey in the foreword to his hugely popular, genre-defining 1989 book *The 7 Habits Of Highly Effective People*.) Both these thoughts suggest that success is something that is worked towards, not necessarily achieved. But they don't answer another question: how does one feel successful? How can you own it?

"Recognition boosts everyone's self-esteem, but learning how to credit and value yourself without needing the presence of others is very helpful," says Ms Mary Spillane, a London-based executive coach who has worked with businesses including the BBC, IBM and BMW. "Many people don't hear praise and therefore don't feel the recognition they have earned. Others don't need to feel successful and are driven by other things: learning, growing, doing something new, or for others."

So, potentially, it's about goals, rather than recognition, per se. The thing about goals, though, is that it's not always clear what they mean, or who is defining them. This is what struck me when, for the purposes of this piece, I started asking my friends about success. The most interesting conversation was with a man – let's call him Mr Smith – who, in his first job, became the top performer at a recruitment firm in the City. If anyone should have a feeling of having achieved goals, I thought, it would be him. But he says this early, goal-driven employment was something of a nightmare. "The sole focus was to produce revenue," he says. "Our targets were annual, monthly, weekly, daily and, I kid you not, hourly. I set myself the target of becoming top biller and then I'd allow myself to quit."

He made the target, but didn't quit – after meeting his personal goal, he felt a responsibility to the company, to work harder to keep others afloat. In fact, he didn't leave until the pressure he felt led him to develop severe, physical anxiety symptoms. "At no point did I find my early success in my industry galvanising," he says. "All I wanted each week/month was to have my head above water and not let management down."

Mr Smith now runs his own profitable business in the same sector. It's enabled him to focus on what is important to him – delivering satisfaction to clients, nurturing colleagues and sharing the fruits of success with the whole business in the form of benefits, such as "more freedom" and "more flexibility" – words you never see in a Google analytics report.

Apparently, meeting goals, in and of itself, doesn't necessarily lead to that feeling that we might conjure when we hear the word "success". This is where all the metrics can become a little disheartening. They are informative, certainly; indicative, maybe. But are they meaningful? In her book *How To Be Happy At Work*, Ms Annie McKee argues that workers (and by inference, people) should focus on "vision", not "goals", despite what is written on their HR-approved performance plan. "In our hypercompetitive, achievement-oriented workplaces, setting and achieving goals has become the main event," she writes, "not something we do on the road to something bigger and more meaningful."

And here's the crux of it: in our data-driven world we tend to mix up "success" with "meaning" – or rather, feel more comfortable with the former word, when what we really are looking for is the latter quality. You can see why. "Success", as a concept, like "data" seems business-y, hard, scientific. "Meaning", seems floaty, self-help-y, even self-indulgent. Perhaps because one is measured externally, while the other is measured personally. But really, they are the same thing: a feeling that what you are doing is worthwhile. The difficulty, of course, is that while your computer can tell you how many visits you've had on your website, it can't tell you why you should care. That part is up to you – an awful responsibility. But one that, you have to agree, seems far more worthy of your time than whatever spreadsheet is currently lurking in your inbox. Doesn't it?

How to:

DRESS FOR WORK

Traditional business attire may be falling rapidly out of fashion, but it remains a fact that most of us still need to dress for work. Being properly presented is part of professionalism; we do it for the comfort of our clients, our customers and our patients. And though costume varies from industry to industry and job to job, there are a few universal rules that it'll benefit you to know, regardless of whether you work on the city, in Silicon Valley or anywhere in between.

THE GROUND RULES

Stick to the script

If there is such a thing as a dress code in your office, do your utmost to treat it with respect. By following the rules you're letting your employer and colleagues know you're part of the team. This advice is especially relevant to the world of finance, one of the last remaining bastions of the corporate dress code. But it's worth keeping in mind wherever you work.

Consider your audience

A question to ask every morning is not what you'll be doing, but who you'll be seeing. How you dress is a powerful form of non-verbal communication, so consider the message your outfit sends. Expensive suits might win you favour with clients on Wall Street, but won't go down so well if you're a doctor.

Develop a system

If you work a standard, nine-to-five, five-days-a-week kind of job – no straightforward assumption in this modern age of digital nomadism – then you're going to need an easily replicable formula. Commit to memory at least five outfits that you know work well, and make sure they're all clean, pressed and ready to go before Monday rolls around.

Be yourself

Copying someone's look at work is risky. Some will love it; imitation is the sincerest form of flattery, after all. Others will see it as too close for comfort, or worse, a statement of competition. So wear the stuff you genuinely like. As long as it doesn't stray beyond dress codes, it'll help you to stand out – people are drawn to those with a sense of individuality.

Don't neglect comfort

We spend a great deal of our waking lives at work, so however you choose to dress, keep in mind you'll be wearing those clothes for the rest of the day. It might be worth making a few concessions to comfort, especially if you have a long or arduous commute. Why not keep your shoes at work and wear something more comfortable for the journey?

THE DETAILS

The hair

Such are the neuroses inherent in most workplaces that people tend to overstyle their hair. Be careful: it should be neat, but not too neat, tamed with product, but not (shudder) crispy. Not that this is the only way, but the predominant "do" in the MR PORTER office is a short back and sides, the fringe swept back and held in place with some low-shine matt wax.

The jacket

A jacket isn't as vital a garment as, say, a pair of trousers, in that you could feasibly get away with leaving the house without one. This is exactly why you should wear a jacket, to elevate your outfit above the base level of acceptable public attire. A chore jacket, unstructured blazer or lightweight bomber would work nicely in less formal office environments.

The shirt

If you work in the kind of establishment that still expects its workers to wear a tie, you'll no doubt already have a selection of cotton-poplin shirts in various shades of white and blue. Less formal office? You might prefer an Oxford shirt instead. Its collar is softer and less starched than that of a formal shirt, so it looks more natural when worn without a tie.

The chinos

Can you wear shorts to work? Sweatpants? A skirt? We've been asked these questions multiple times, and every time our response is the same: it depends. On your job, your boss, your colleagues, your city... A better question might be: what are the most appropriate trousers for a smart-casual office? Our suggestion: a pair of slim-fitted chinos in navy or tan.

The shoes

It's a truism that shoes are the first thing people notice about you, but the reason truisms become truisms in the first place is because they're, well... true. If you want to make the right impression in the workplace, start by looking at what you wear on your feet. Our advice? Invest in a couple of pairs of Goodyear-welted Derbies and take care of them.

5

HEALTH IN MIND

HOW TO TALK TO YOUR FRIENDS ABOUT THE THINGS THAT MATTER

Five ways to move your
conversation beyond banter

Words by Mr Oliver Burkeman

LOOK FOR THE SIGNS

When it comes to personal problems, the stereotype is that men favour a clear, logical, rational approach. But that can be a barrier when you, or a friend, can't fully express what's wrong, due either to embarrassment or to sheer lack of self-understanding. So it's crucial to trust your intuition, whether you're seeking help or offering it. Are you feeling inexplicably sad, or engaging in unhealthy behaviour more often than usual? Do you get the sense that a friend needs to talk, even if he can't say so? It's tempting to think of gut feelings as squishy, unreliable things, but they evolved precisely as a way for our brains to process massive amounts of information, about facial expressions and other non-verbal cues, much faster than we'd manage via conscious deliberation.

ONLY CONNECT

Don't get hung up about having emotional conversations in the "right" way. Most of the benefit comes from having them at all, although it's better to have them face to face rather than online, when possible, since large swathes of interpersonal communication are non-verbal. Being too self-conscious about whether you're correctly following certain steps can only get in the way. You don't even necessarily need to talk explicitly about personal problems. You can connect deeply while speaking about sport, or work, or travel, provided you approach the interaction in an emotionally open frame of mind. And if a friend is in pain, you needn't worry that talking might make things worse. We sometimes fear reminding others of their distress, for example after a bereavement, but studies suggest that's rarely a factor. They won't need reminding, and they'll probably be happy to unburden themselves.

FOLLOW THE FIVE PER CENT RULE

A large body of psychological research shows that friendships get deeper via disclosure reciprocity: I tell you something a bit personal, then you match it with something equally personal, and so on, in a back-and-forth process. People who never reciprocate come across as aloof, but people who suddenly vent all their deepest feelings at once risk freaking everyone out. To overcome the awkwardness of emotional conversation, a useful guide is to nudge yourself out of your comfort zone by about five per cent. If you're talking to someone you've only ever bantered with before, now isn't the time to reveal your trauma-filled childhood or ask why their marriage collapsed. But it might be the moment to mention, say, how stressful you're finding work these days. Still, don't sweat this to the point of becoming self-conscious. The main thing is just to talk.

DON'T COMPARE YOUR INSIDES TO OTHER PEOPLE'S OUTSIDES

It's a truth so fundamental that we usually forget it – you only have access to your own inner monologue, not other people's. And so it's almost inevitable that you'll feel as though you're the only one filled with despair, anxiety or self-criticism because yours are the only emotions you ever directly experience. (Impostor syndrome at work is the classic example. You feel like a fraud who's somehow managed to trick everyone into thinking you're qualified, but really they're thinking the same about themselves.) Everyone else might seem as though they have it all together, especially on social media, where we're incentivised to display only the highlights of our lives, but the truth is that, from their perspective, you probably seem like you've got it all together, too. Never refrain from starting a conversation because you fear you're the only person in distress. You almost certainly aren't and, in many cases, your willingness to go first in admitting it will be greeted with grateful relief.

BEWARE THE OVERSHARE

None of this means it's impossible to go too far, to be the too-much-information guy who won't stop yammering about his feelings, or to become the doormat who's obliged to listen all night to a friend's yammering. The real problem is rarely a matter of too much. What unites the world's genuinely annoying oversharers is that they have a hidden agenda. They're complaining in order to try to make you feel guilty, for example, or to try to get you to give them the specific advice they've already decided they want to hear. Emotional conversations are the most beneficial when all parties let go of any agenda, other than the desire to connect. The best solutions to personal problems generally emerge, unpredictably, from the conversation itself, rather than being imposed on it by one of the participants. We need not completely abandon the strong and silent flavour of masculinity, which at its best embodies a calm confidence in one's ability to navigate the world. We just need the confidence to navigate the world of emotions, too.

FIVE WAYS TO
PRACTISE SELF-CARE

Words by Mr Ahmed Zambarakji

Of all the touchy-feely terms that have sprung from the wellness movement, self-care ranks high on the cringe spectrum. On the surface, the idea of prioritising our well-being reeks of self-indulgence. But if modern psychology has taught us anything, it's that we're of no use to anyone – employer, family or friends – if we don't carve out time to maintain our physical, emotional and mental health. In fact, the more you invest in your career, the more you need to invest in self-care.

As a yoga teacher and healer, I'm often confronted with clients who have compromised their health in order to secure success. My job is to remind them that well-being and accomplishment are not mutually exclusive. There is no one-size-fits-all solution. One person's silent Buddhist retreat is another person's hell. A seven-course tasting menu might seem healing to you, but a gluttonous nightmare to your neighbour. Gym time works for some gents; nap time works for others.

The easier it is to implement a routine, the more likely it is to become a habit and have a long-term impact. With that in mind, here are five quick methods to help you hit the reset button on life – practices I encourage my clients to incorporate into their busy lives as often as possible.

SPEND TIME IN NATURE

The intensity and buzz of a city are as exhausting as they are exciting. And while our nervous system and brain can withstand the incessant stream of stimuli, neither fares particularly well if we don't find time to pause.

Calling a time-out to convene with nature is an easy and pleasant antidote to modern life, and science is starting to validate its power. A leisurely stroll through the park during your lunch break will shift brainwaves from the beta state to alpha. Put simply, this means that the chemical and electrical signals in your grey matter go from the waking state (analysing, planning, compartmentalising) to the lucid state, where reflection, understanding and relaxation come to the fore. This is the "present moment" that meditation and yoga aim to cultivate.

With alpha waves, the brain is more adept at finding creative solutions to problems. And, just like during meditation, there is a measurable drop in heart rate, blood pressure and stress hormones. The best part is that this ritual requires very little of you. All you have to do is find a green area (and leave your phone behind).

EMPTY YOUR MIND

I often meet clients and students who feel like they have failed at meditation. The reason for their dismay is that their thoughts – pesky things – keep on coming whenever they sit down to meditate. Sometimes they race even more ferociously.

A complete silencing of the mind on their first few attempts is overly optimistic and testament to the general level of misunderstanding about meditation. The practice is in observing the mind rather than expecting it to shut up immediately.

The good news is there are other, ways to empty your brain first thing in the morning. One technique I often champion is Morning Pages, a form of automatic writing pioneered by Ms Julia Cameron, an American artist and author of *The Artist's Way*. As the name suggests, the technique involves writing three pages of longhand, stream-of-consciousness notes the moment you wake up.

Morning Pages can be about anything, from the mundane to the philosophical. The point is that you empty your brain onto the page in an immediate and organic fashion without any preamble. It is astonishing to see what the unconscious mind coughs up, and the mental space created will bring relief.

GET PHYSICAL

Increased awareness around mental health has significantly undone the stigma around talking therapies for men. Verbalising stress or trauma was once considered weak. Today, it's considered being human.

And while people make great strides in therapy, I also recommend getting out of your head and back into your body. Finding a physical, that is to say a somatic, connection to your emotions tends to provide a profound sense of relief.

Yoga, therapeutic touch, massage and bodywork (think hands-on healing or, if you need to be kneaded, Rolfing, Hellerwork, shiatsu or myofascial release) all distract the machinations of the mind by tapping in to visceral feelings. These therapies hinge on the premise that our life experiences are imprinted in the body, in the muscles, cells, bones and fascia, rather than somewhere in the brain. Physically massaging them out helps you work through and release pain and negativity.

If that sounds too passive for you, you can always destroy a punchbag.

CREATE FOR CREATIVITY'S SAKE

As children, play was part and parcel of life. It was a way of developing physical, cognitive and emotional strength while having fun. It didn't have an end game and, for the most part, it wasn't competitive. The expression of creativity was its own reward.

As adults, financial and social responsibilities inevitably take up our precious free time and, before long, the guitar that saw you through adolescence is collecting dust in the corner. That brilliant screenplay? Never wrote it. Paints and charcoals are tossed in the bin. We've become logical, linear, and even a bit boring.

Giving tangible form to an idea or impulse is not just therapeutic, it is a meditative practice that expands our perception of the world. Our environment shifts from black and white to technicolour and, in this state, we feel more connected and alive.

The dividends from creativity, whatever shape it takes, are manifold. One article published in *Scientific American* even suggests that creativity predicts a longer life because "creative thinking reduces stress and keeps the brain healthy". And because this creative pursuit isn't supposed to be profitable, you don't even have to be good at it.

ACTS OF SERVICE

One potentially negative side effect of practising self-care is that many people end up disappearing down a "me first" rabbit hole. At some point, our inner journey should reflect the way in which we interact with others. For those who have disappeared up their own backside, action in the form of charity is the best medicine.

Every community needs volunteers – in soup kitchens, in care homes – and people who are willing to raise awareness for a greater cause. We live in a world of social injustice, economic disparity and isolation, and the most effective remedy for these maladies is human connection.

The very act of reaching out to another person recognises that we are not separate. To wit, helping others is, in some metaphysical fashion, a way of helping ourselves. Most importantly, witnessing another person's struggle will almost certainly put first-world problems into perspective.

HEALTHY HOLIDAYS AROUND THE WORLD

The top destinations that combine kicking back with body maintenance

Words by Ms Gemma Bowes

FINN LOUGH *Northern Ireland (opposite)*

Best for: nature-lovers

One of the most interesting retreats we've seen, Finn Lough is a serene rural escape beside Lough Erne that has an intriguing Element Trail private wellness experience. Guests walk through woodland between cabins, each one of which offers a different treatment, such as a salt bath, Finnish sauna, hydrotherapy pool and a hot tub overlooking the bay.

There's a quirky approach to the accommodation, too, which comprises a collection of transparent bubble domes, in which guests can fall asleep looking up at starry skies. There are also modern lakeside cottages with white panelling and wood burners for those who like more privacy and a real roof over their heads. Tennis, fishing, boating and kayaking fill up the rest of your stay.

ALILA YANGSHUO *China*

Best for: climbing

Alila Yangshuo, a converted sugar mill set among the karst rock formations of Guangxi Province, is jaw-droppingly beautiful – a place for switching off and getting outdoors. Most dramatic is the outdoor pool built onto a platform over a river, from which sugar used to be loaded onto cargo boats.

The spa is like nothing you've seen before, set underground in what looks like a designer cave, reminiscent of the Tate Modern Tanks. Specialist Asian treatments, such as a Balinese massage with black sugar, are the focus, while the hotel can arrange rock climbing on the iconic limestone crags, hiking and mountain biking. Being wholly abstemious here would be something of a waste, considering there's an on-site rum distillery whose produce is put to delicious use in the 1969 Bar.

YÄAN WELLNESS *Mexico*

Best for: chilling out

Tulum has become the go-to beach spot for bohemians everywhere, from Brixton to Berlin. Yäan Wellness is one of the more recent openings and has all the roughly hewn bare wood, overhanging palms and mid-century furniture you might expect, though the addition of a concrete-clad indoor pool, black marble worktops and deep copper baths takes it to the next level.

The retreat's signature treatments, such as a monthly Moon Temazcal (sweat lodge), take inspiration from indigenous traditions and include massages that involve the whispering of sacred chants. Urban cynicism should be checked at the door. One of its founders, clinical psychologist Dr Bobby Klein, studied with Tibetan Buddhists and Native American tribes and is deeply influenced by their ancient approach to well-being.

SHAKTI HIMALAYA *India*

Best for: altitude training

Shakti Himalaya's epic adventure holidays immerse travellers in the culture and staggering scenery of three mountain states: Sikkim, Ladakh and at Kumaon in Uttarakhand. In places of intense beauty intended to soothe the soul, these trips aim to teach you about living on the roof of the world. With trekking altitudes of 3,500 to 4,200m, you are sure to get a boost to strength and stamina, too, as athletes will testify.

Trips are largely tailor-made and can include one or all three destinations, but they typically involve daily hikes between remote villages with guides, chefs and porters. Accommodation is in traditional village houses and luxury tented camps.

Examples include a Ladakh Village Experience holiday in the mountain villages of the Indus Valley, or the Head In The Clouds mindfulness retreat, which entails morning Buddhist meditation and prayers with monks, silent hikes that feature stops for meditation and yoga at mountain beauty spots, plus a stay at Shakti 360 Leti, the outfit's luxury lodge.

NIHI SUMBA ISLAND *Indonesia*

Best for: surfing

Even people new to surfing know that Indonesia is a land of promise. Waves from the gentlest beginner-friendly ripples to huge turquoise barrels are par for the course, and riding sessions are followed by balmy nights under coconut palms. The country has a wide choice of surf camps, but Nihi Sumba Island blows the others out of the water with its world-class surf school and decadent villas decked out in Balinese carvings and boasting canopy beds, private pools and hot tubs.

Created in 1984 as a tropical surf camp with a bohemian vibe, it was bought in 2012 by Mr Christopher Burch and Mr James McBride, former MD of The Carlyle Hotel in New York. They gave it a $15m revamp, which kept the laid-back spirit while raising the quality of catering and service to industry-leading standards.

A big sell is Sumba's "private" wave, Occy's Left, one of the world's most famous barrels, which only 10 surfers a day get a chance to ride. To calm down, there's yoga and a spa safari to a private cliff-side space.

HOW TO ALWAYS GET A GOOD NIGHT'S SLEEP

The experts give us the low-down on how to get the best shut-eye possible

Words by Mr Alfred Tong

Every one of us needs good sleep to ensure we look, feel and perform at our best. And yet, although we're aware of its manifold benefits, the vestiges of a macho dismissal of sleep as dead time linger on. The cliché of the superhuman CEO or politician who needs only four hours per night still abounds. But now this attitude looks to be on its way out.

Not long ago, The Rand Corporation calculated the economic cost of America's 1.2 million working days per year lost to poor sleep at $411bn. In Japan – where 60 per cent of the populace get fewer than the seven hours required to stave off a 35 per cent higher mortality risk – the annual tally is $138bn. In the UK, overtired employees reportedly cost the economy $50bn a year. All those figures are predicted to rise.

Thankfully, a recent cultural shift driven by the burgeoning wellness industry has resulted in a decent night's sleep increasingly being viewed as a vital signifier of a healthy mind and body. According to the 2017 McKinsey report, the US sleep market – including all those coveted mattresses, weighted blankets and white-noise machines – is worth between $30bn and $40bn and is expected to snowball in coming decades. Indeed, a cursory Google search reveals a plethora of self-professed sleep gurus offering various services and gizmos.

"It's great that more people are interested in sleep, but it's a relatively new field of research and I fear that anyone can be a 'sleep expert'," says Dr Chris Winter, a neurologist of 26 years and author of *The Sleep Solution*. Dr Neil Stanley, who has published 38 peer-reviewed papers on sleep research, says: "Advice on how to sleep better is pretty much all common sense." It is, however, not quite common enough. So, here is how to get a good night's sleep, according to the people who really know.

INVEST IN A GOOD BED

According to Mr Simon Williams, marketing manager of the National Bed Federation, you need to replace your mattress at least once every seven years. "Tell-tale signs that you need a new bed include: waking up with a sore back or neck, the sound of creaks and crunches when you move around, the feeling of springs and ridges, uneven sagging, stains and tears on the mattress." Finding the right bed for you is a matter of trial and error, and it's best to lie in a bed for at least 10 minutes before deciding. "It's quite subjective, and it's often down to personal preference and body size and weight," says Ms Jessica Alexander, spokesperson for The Sleep Council. "While comfort is a matter of personal preference, your bed must be hard enough to give proper support to your spine and body. A 6ft tall, 18-stone person may need something more robust than someone who is 8 stone. When it comes to materials, quality and durability, on the whole, you get what you pay for. Always try before you buy and avoid the temptation to buy a mattress online." Dr Stanley agrees. "A good bed is worth more than the cost of an iPhone," he says.

MANIPULATE YOUR CIRCADIAN RHYTHMS

"Very few people actually have insomnia," says Dr Winter. "What's more common is that people are struggling to sleep when they want to in order to do their jobs or live the life they want."

People are either "night owls" or "morning larks", which means they have a genetically determined preference for mornings or evenings. Dr Winter believes that, with the use of light and exercise, it's possible for night owls to cope better with early mornings. "For instance, a regular 6.00am bike ride will help your body advance its sleep cycle and over time it will become easier to wake in the morning."

STICK TO A SCHEDULE

You can also manipulate your circadian rhythms using intelligent lightbulbs (Dr Winter recommends a brand called Soraa). These emit blue light in the morning to rejuvenate and energise you, and gradually softening white light in the evening to help prepare you for bed. "Melatonin – the hormone that regulates sleep – interacts with different colours of light to influence sleep cycles," says Dr Winter. "When you're trying to reset your sleep cycle, it's important to stick to a consistent schedule, just as parents do with babies." Dr Stanley also believes that consistency is key. "Your body craves routine and predictability," he says. "The more you chop and change your sleep time, the more confused your body will become. I'm in bed by 9.30pm every night, as I know this is the time I need to sleep in order to wake up early." In addition, ensure you stick to regular mealtimes and exercise sessions as this will also help to set sleep rhythms.

THAT MEANS AT
THE WEEKEND, TOO

The first third of a night's sleep is the deepest and most restorative, and the latter two-thirds comprise lighter, yet still restorative, sleep categorised as stage 2. Sleepers typically pass through five stages: 1, 2, 3, 4 and REM (rapid eye movement) sleep. "Have you ever noticed that you wake up before your alarm clock goes off?" asks Dr Stanley. "That's because your body knows when you're about to wake and starts to prepare 90 minutes before you wake up. That's why it's essential to stick to a routine."

Unfortunately, this means no lie-ins at the weekend as this would confuse matters come Monday morning. And definitely do not hit the snooze button. "You're better off setting your alarm for the latest possible time and make sure you definitely get up at that time," says Dr Stanley. "Hitting snooze confuses the body further, making it even more difficult to get up."

SLEEP ALONE

"It is far better to sleep alone," says Dr Stanley. "You can have kisses and cuddles before retiring to your own bed. It's only very recently that society decided it was a sign of a close relationship to sleep in the same bed as our partner." Differing sleep patterns (your partner might be a night owl and you a morning lark), snoring, sleep talking, increased temperature from the other person's body and less room can also mean that sleep may be disturbed.

"A standard UK double bed measures 4ft 6in, whereas a standard UK single bed measures 2ft 6in," says Dr Stanley. "This means an adult sleeping in a double bed with their partner gets 3in less space than the average child sleeping in a single bed."

KEEP YOUR COOL

"In order to sleep, your body needs to lose 1ºC of temperature," says Dr Stanley. "Carbon dioxide also disturbs sleep, so try to sleep with a window and bedroom door open all year round. The room temperature should be between 16 and 18ºC. If you're cold, it is better to keep the bed warm with a hot-water bottle and have the window open slightly."

Central heating can raise room temperature to 20 to 24ºC, the point at which it becomes uncomfortable to sleep. Synthetic foam beds, which are often sold as premium products, do not regulate heat as effectively and can lead to overheating, as can pillows and duvets made from cheap, synthetic fibres. Dr Stanley advises using products made from 100 per cent natural cotton, feather or wool to help regulate bed temperature and prevent overheating.

Eating your main evening meal three or four hours before bedtime is also essential. If you leave it too late, your body will still be working to digest the meal and won't have cooled down by that essential 1ºC.

BAN DEVICES FROM THE BEDROOM

Blue-light pollution, which is emitted from the screens of electronic devices, disturbs the production of melatonin and can trick the brain into thinking it's still daytime. Although you can now get blue-light-blocking glasses, this does not mean it's OK to binge-watch a boxset into the early hours. The cognitive stimulation from the excitement of a Netflix marathon does not make for a restful night's shut-eye. Ideally, invest in a proper alarm clock – don't use the one on your phone –and make a point of keeping laptops, tablets and mobiles out of your bedroom.

NB, IT'S PERSONAL

"The amount of sleep you need is mainly down to genetics," says Dr Stanley. "Generally speaking, you need between six and nine hours of sleep a night. The problem with the eight-hour figure is that it causes anxiety if people are sleeping for more or less. The amount of sleep you need is determined by how you feel during the day. If you feel awake and alert, then you're getting enough sleep. I like to get nine-and-a-half hours." Dr Winter agrees. "Everyone is slightly different," he says. "Sleep duration is genetically determined. Eight hours is an arbitrary figure, a nice round number, but when it comes to sleep, you cannot have a one-size-fits-all approach."

QUIET MIND, RESTED BODY

According to the World Health Organization, the average noise outside your bedroom window should not exceed 40 decibels, similar to that of a library, otherwise you won't get a decent night's sleep. Long-term average exposure to levels above 55 decibels, about the same as a busy street, contributes to elevated blood pressure and even heart attacks.

"A quiet mind and rested body are essential for a good night's sleep," says Dr Stanley. "So whether it's meditating, yoga, having a warm bath or settling any arguments you might have had, make sure you are nice and relaxed before bed. Never go to bed angry or worried."

MR JON HAMM IS IN A BETTER PLACE NOW

The Hollywood actor on why everyone sometimes needs a little help to get them through the day

Words by Mr Richard Godwin

Mr Jon Hamm, photographed in Los Angeles by Mr Tomo Brejc

I t's a sunny day in LA. Seeing as I was coming to meet the man who's done more to raise sartorial standards than just about any other living male – did anyone wear a pocket square pre-*Mad Men*? – I've decided to sport a nice linen jacket and tassel loafers. But Mr Jon Hamm is dressed down in an NHL cap, a red, white and blue checked shirt, dark jeans and Converse, plus a couple of days of stubble. "Jesus, you look so smart," he says. "I look like a suburban dad who's got lost on the way to school."

He has spent longer in LA than anywhere else and, well, there have been ups and downs. But of the ups, the eight years he spent on *Mad Men* – Mr Matthew Weiner's drama set in a 1960s New York ad agency – threaten to reduce everything else to a footnote. As he is all too aware.

This is the man who played Don Draper, the most iconic male in perhaps the most iconic show in the Golden Age of TV. He's the man who recalibrated masculinity, who repopularised the old fashioned, whom women wanted to bed and men wanted to be, even though everyone knew he was selling a lie, who was, in Mr Hamm's words, "a fundamentally fucked-up human being". He's among the most objectified males on the planet. "It is not easy having immediate and huge-scale fame thrust upon you. I'm a pretty shy person. I like talking to people one-on-one, but I do not like people taking pictures of me with 400mm lenses across the street. It's mystifying to me why we give that any time in our culture."

Soon after the series ended, Mr Hamm split with his partner of 18 years, the film actor/director Ms Jennifer Westfeldt, and checked into rehab for alcoholism. Around that time, *The New York Times* asked: "Is there life after Don Draper?"

Let's hope so. Mr Hamm is not only one of the most likeable stars in Hollywood – he says he owes his career breaks mainly to being "nice", respectful of people's time, listening, preparing – he's also a damn fine actor, belatedly honoured with an Emmy for that final season.

There's a certain Midwestern modesty to him. He makes it clear that his relationship is not up for discussion ("It's very personal and specific and I think people tend to draw their own conclusions about that anyway"), but the implication is that he's single. However, he's upfront about almost everything else including the moment he has to leave for his weekly therapy session. "I find it very helpful," he says.

As for rehab? "It has all these connotations, but it's just an extended period of talking about yourself. People go for all sorts of reasons. There's something to be said for pulling yourself out of the grind for a period of time and concentrating on recalibrating the system. It works. It's great."

Even in his baseball cap, Mr Hamm is as comely as you'd expect from a man whose first credit was "Gorgeous Guy at Bar" in an episode of *Ally McBeal*. One magazine described him as "astronaut handsome", not that astronauts are selected on looks, duh, but it does capture his capable, reassuring, captain-like quality. His voice really does insinuate that everything's going to be OK, but there's something soulful about him, something indefinable that makes you hope he's going to be OK, too.

He lives in Los Feliz, as he has done since he moved to LA, and can often be seen at his local Italian deli, Little Dom's. Is settling down, having kids on the agenda at all? "I don't know. I don't think it's necessarily an imperative. I'm not going to psychoanalyse myself here, but... well, never say never. I've got nieces and nephews and I've been a teacher. I've probably been around kids a lot more than all my friends. I feel if you shut that off entirely you calcify. You turn into *that* guy."

He means the guy who complains about what the kids are up to these days, though he does express a certain bafflement at social media. "I speak to young kids starting out and they can't even get into an audition unless they have a certain number of followers on Instagram. Of course, it doesn't mean anything – you can buy 100,000 followers. But it becomes meaningful if business decides it's meaningful. In time there will be a correction and we will look back and say, 'Wow. We were really dumb.'"

There's a careworn legend that *Mad Men* creator Mr Weiner remarked after his first audition, "Now there's a man who wasn't raised by his parents," which is partly true. Mr Hamm's parents divorced when he was two and his mother, Deborah, died of stomach cancer when he was 10. He moved in with his father, Daniel, a flamboyant character who had sold a trucking business and pursued various jobs, but mostly he was brought up by friends' mothers. "I was always fascinated by my dad because he could talk to anyone. He was a great listener and he knew a little bit about a lot of things. I aspired to be like that."

Happily, he was sent to a school – the private John Burroughs – that pushed a broad curriculum (his mother had put aside her secretary's wages to pay the fees). "In the first couple of years, you were required to take every elective: speech, debate, math, arts, gym." He was good enough at baseball and American football to take them further, but it was drama that he found most rewarding. "I just wasn't that interested in lifting weights all day. Drama was one of the only things I kept coming back to."

Such is his admiration for his school, Mr Hamm returned to teach for a couple of years after finishing at the University of Missouri. By then, his father had died, leaving him an orphan by the age of 20. One of his half-sisters finally convinced him to seek professional help. "After I'd lost my dad, I had this horrible paralysing inertia – and no one in my family was capable of dealing with it. So what do you do? Go and see a professional. I preach it from the mountaintops. I know it's a luxury and not something everyone can afford. But if you can, do it. It's like a mental gym."

At 24, he moved to Los Angeles to give acting a shot. "I decided to give myself until I was 30." Cue several wilderness years of low-rent dramas, waiting tables and even a spell as a set dresser on a porn film, which he says was one of the most depressing experiences of his life.

As he turned 30, he got his first movie: *We Were Soldiers* with Mr Mel Gibson. "I had a small part, but I made a ton of money on it. I thought, OK, I'm working now. I don't have to do a shitty day job any more."

He is reliably damning about the character who eventually made him famous, but does say of Draper, "I guess what was so attractive was this cool confidence. He came from an unstable, strange place, and figured out that he had to project this aura of command and people would follow it."

It's not something that he's taken on – "I'm not interested in fucking with people" – but he does credit Draper with improving his wardrobe. "I don't share a lot of sartorial cues with Mr Draper, other than we're the same suit size, but it did open my eyes to buying clothes that fit properly."

Since then, his big-screen roles have ranged from playing a sports agent in the Disney movie *The Million Dollar Arm* to ex-White House chief of staff, Denis McDonough in 2019's *The Report* with quirkier or comic turns in *Black Mirror*, *30 Rock*, *Good Omens* and *A Young Doctor's Notebook*, opposite Mr Daniel Radcliffe ("I called him and said, 'Hey, if there's anyone who knows how it feels to be defined as one thing, it's me'").

"Once *Mad Men* blew up, it was a conscious decision to pivot away from all that," he says. "It's no secret that I was offered a ton of parts that involved a hat and a cigarette and a glass of brown liquor. But I was like, I do that already. I played Don Draper for 93 episodes – that's enough. If you just want to do the same thing again and again, why get into acting?"

Still, I sense a frustration when it comes to more serious films. "It's really difficult. There are only so many slots. There are five or six leads who get the first look and if you're lucky you might get a second."

As we close the conversation, we move on to his hometown of St Louis and the unrest. "Police violence is such a difficult thing to comprehend. If you sat me next to a black person who had also grown up in St Louis, simply by the nature of the colour of our skin, we're going to have completely different experiences. It's so difficult for people to grasp as it rams up against our ideas of fairness and authority. The more and more shit that comes out like this, it's harder and harder for people to dismiss."

But he hopes good will come from it. "I'm an optimist. I think the more we find out, the more the culture will shift. I hate this idea that nothing matters. It can't all be a dumbshow." He stops himself. "Sorry, that got real dark real quick," he apologises. Something Don Draper would *never* do.

How to:

CHILL OUT IN STYLE

For those rare evenings (or mornings or afternoons – or even minutes) when you find yourself commitment-free, donning proper leisurewear is a vital act of self-care and central to the age-old philosophy of "me-time". And it's not just about softer and cosier fabrics – the act of shrugging off the day (and pulling on something slightly more appealing, preferably in cashmere) is as much a balm for the mind as it is the body. Here's how to do airplane mode right.

THE GROUND RULES

Make time

The first rule of relaxing: you're not going to be able to do it unless you actually clear some space for it. That means scheduling in time to do nothing. A bit of aimlessness once in a while is not only harmless, but alleviates stress and boosts creativity.

Out with the old

Every man has a favourite old T-shirt or pair of grey sweatpants that he's had in his possession since time immemorial. Bad news: while you might find this garment comforting, the world at large finds it... deeply unpleasant. Do your friends and loved ones a favour and refrain from wearing anything with holes, indelible stains or mysterious odours, no matter how poignant it may feel to you.

Prepare for surprises

It's inevitably when you're at your most slovenly and ungroomed that a family member decides to pop round. Or someone sets off the fire alarm. Or you have to nip out to the shops for a vital ingredient. Build your loungewear around the idea that you may have to present yourself to the outside world at short notice. As in: keep it clean, and keep it decent.

Read the label

What separates loungewear from normalwear? The fabric. And the best way to ensure you're getting enough stretchiness and silkiness is to look at its composition. Cashmere and alpaca add softness. Knit linen has a silky feel. So, obviously, does silk. You may not like elastane and spandex in jeans, but, for sweatpants, these can be comfortable additions.

Think big

Of course, relaxing isn't just a mode of dress, but a state of mind. If you want to really get there, we would recommend putting down your phone, switching off the television, lighting a pleasantly scented candle, closing your eyes and letting your thoughts drift over you like clouds across the sky. Now, doesn't that sound relaxing?

THE DETAILS

The headphones

Some of us live in blissful rural landscapes, and others – many – of us live in horrible cities full of noise and smog and people screaming and cars honking. That's why a proper pair of noise-cancelling headphones are a pre-requisite for any serious relaxation session. We like Bang & Olufsen's H9i set. What to listen to? Search iTunes for *The MR PORTER Podcast* – surely the most stylishly relaxing podcast out there. (And yes, we have to say that.)

The eye mask

They may have slightly princess-y connotations, but, by gum, if you're going to get a nap on-demand, on your own terms, you need one of these. Silk varieties are particularly kind to the skin and help to avoid the startled panda look on waking.

The shawl-neck cardigan

Find the right combination of fibres (see ground rules) and the right chunkiness of knit (essentially: chunky) and wearing one of these is like being given a giant hug. Plus, they look good – just Google Mr Steve McQueen if you need any convincing of that fact.

The cashmere sweatpants

Cashmere and sweatpants are like strawberries and ice cream. Individually, they're wonderful, but together, they are sublime. In the summer, you may want to swap these for a merino wool or knit cotton variety, but in the colder months of the year, you won't come close to anything else for superlative comfort.

The wool socks

If you go to a yoga or meditation class, they're likely to tell you to relax from the crown of your head to the tips of your toes. And the same goes for furnishing yourself with loungewear. Sort of. OK, yes, you don't need cable-knit, wool socks, but, now you know they exist, don't you want some? The slouchier and chunkier the better.

6

NOURISHMENT

WINE TASTING MADE EASY

Here's a crash course in knowing what's flowing down your gullet

Words by Mr Chris Elvidge

Wine: it's one of those areas in which most of us have a wealth of experience, but very little expertise. In an attempt to correct this, we've put together the following bluffer's guide. No, it won't turn you into the world's greatest sommelier, but yes, it might help you explain what all that sniffing and swishing is all about.

WATCH THE TEMPERATURE

Chilling a wine that shouldn't be chilled – or neglecting to chill one that should – can have a profound effect on its aroma, alcohol content and acidity. At higher temperatures, the evaporation rate of volatile compounds on the surface of the wine increases, making it noticeably more aromatic and alcoholic on the nose. At lower temperatures, these aromas are dulled, allowing acidic and tannic notes to come to the fore. It's reductive to suggest that red wines are best served at room temperature. Certain reds, such as beaujolais nouveau, drink very well indeed when chilled. Certain whites, too, taste better when they're not ice-cold. Oaked chardonnay is perhaps the most cited example of a white wine that benefits from a few minutes out of the fridge before drinking. In short, treat each wine individually, do your research and, if in doubt, use a thermometer.

GET THE RIGHT GLASSWARE

A good wine glass should have a large bowl that narrows towards the top, which serves to collect and concentrate the wine's aromatic compounds as they rise towards your nose. (The point of a large glass is not to hold more wine, but to achieve a larger surface area for evaporation. For this reason, you should only fill your glass to its widest part, not up to the top.) Invest in all-purpose wine glasses first. It's possible to buy ones that are shaped to bring out the characteristic aromas of certain types of wine – and in some cases even certain grapes – but this is an unnecessary step for all but the most committed oenophiles. The only other piece of glassware you really need, then, is a decanter, which helps to soften overly tannic wines and is vital for older vintages, which may have developed a layer of sediment in the bottom of the bottle.

HAVE A GOOD SNIFF

A large part of the taste of any given wine is down to its aroma, so make sure you smell it before you drink it. There are dozens of different aroma compounds that can be contained within a bottle of wine, from fresh and floral to earthy and vegetal. These are categorised as primary (originating from the grapes and the soil), secondary (developed during fermentation) or tertiary aromas (developed as the wine ages). Understanding how to first identify and then describe these aromas is crucial to wine tasting. It helps, of course, to know what you're looking for in the first place. Wines made from the cabernet sauvignon grape, for instance, are known to contain the distinct aroma of green peppers; gewürztraminer has the recognisable aroma of lychee; young pinot noir smells of strawberries; Australian shiraz is known for its spicy aromas of black pepper and liquorice; and so on. Committing a few of these to memory will make things a lot easier in the long run.

TAKE A SIP

Now is the time to actually drink the wine. As you take your first mouthful, swirl it around your mouth, allowing it to make contact with all parts of your tongue, and ask yourself some crucial questions. Is it sweet or dry? (If you're unsure, hold your nose – the smell can be distracting.) How much crispness or acidity can you detect? Does it have a high concentration of tannins? (These are the chemical compounds found in the skin of a grape that give certain wines their mouth-drying astringency. They're most clearly felt as a roughness on your gums.) One more thing to analyse at this point is the body of a wine. In layman's terms, this means how thick a liquid it is. The classic comparison: a light-bodied wine will have the consistency of skimmed milk, while a full-bodied wine will have a heavier, creamier feel in the mouth.

WHERE FOOD MEETS ART

What patron chef Mr Massimo Bottura
is cooking up at Osteria Francescana

Words by Mr Tom M Ford

Previous page and above: Mr Massimo Bottura at Osteria Francescana, Modena.
Below: Oops! I Dropped The Lemon Tart at Osteria Francescana

I t was an achievement more than 20 years in the making. At The World's 50 Best Restaurants Awards in New York, 2016, Osteria Francescana was finally named the number one restaurant on Earth – knocking El Celler de Can Roca off the top spot and becoming the first Italian establishment to take the title. In 2018, after being briefly eclipsed by Manhattan's Eleven Madison Park, owner Mr Massimo Bottura triumphed once again. Long recognised as one of the world's greatest chefs, he gained his third Michelin star in 2012, and Osteria has been hovering around the world's top five since 2011. It has not always been like this, however. When Mr Bottura opened his restaurant in 1995 in his birthplace of Modena – a quaint, pastel-hued city in Emilia-Romagna, Northern Italy – the locals (and the food critics) did not take kindly to him tampering with the time-honoured dishes that their mammas and nonnas used to make. Misunderstood for the first five years of business, he nearly gave it all up.

You can appreciate why the residents of Modena – home to the finest (and fastest) Italian supercar makers, but equally renowned for slow cooking and even slower pace of life – were reluctant to accept Mr Bottura. Meeting him in his restaurant, he speaks almost as fast as he drives his Maserati, launching into lengthy speeches about the concept of creativity and his cultural influences. These range from travel to poetry to music. But it is contemporary art that has had the most apparent impact on his food. Oops! I Dropped The Lemon Tart, for example, is a dish that was inspired when his chef, Taka, did exactly that. Mr Bottura insisted that they recreate it on the plate. The restaurant itself is adorned with contemporary art: a piece by Mr Maurizio Cattelan shows two pigeons defecating on the classic art of previous generations – a metaphor representing Mr Bottura's own desire to "break the past". "It's saying, 'Come on guys, let's move to the 21st century and start seeing things with new eyes.' It's not to be disrespectful," he says.

Indeed, Mr Bottura has always respected his roots. This is something that is crucial for any Italian chef even today. He thinks that parmigiano reggiano, the granular cheese unique to the region, is "the most valuable ingredient". He talks lovingly about the philosophy of Italian food – the "slow passages of time in the ageing process. The secret of the food valley where I live." And, above all, he loves Modena. "There is a script from the 13th century called *The Decameron*, by Giovanni Boccaccio. He came from Florence to Modena and he wrote about it as this amazing place with beautiful women sitting on mountains of grated cheese making pasta 24 hours a day. That's Modena! It's the secret of life. And it hasn't changed in 700 years."

For Mr Bottura's passatelli recipe, see p. 220

HOW TO COOK WITH FIRE

Super-chef Mr Francis Mallmann
shares his tips for the perfect
flame-grilled steak

Words by Mr Samuel Muston

That the Argentine chef Mr Francis Mallmann has never used a microwave will come as no surprise to people who saw his bravura performance on Netflix's *Chef's Table*. Sure, he may be the most famous cook in the southern hemisphere and, yes, he spent a fair chunk of the late 20th century working in Parisian restaurants, but Mr Mallmann is a dyed-in-the-wool eccentric with a taste for the romantic. You are as likely to find him operating a Zanussi oven as you are to find a whale operating a power shower. He prefers earthier means of cooking. He likes the crackle of wood and open flames, as any of his 600,000+ Instagram followers (including avowed fan Mr David Beckham) can attest. He now has restaurants in Uruguay, Argentina, the US and the latest in France, where he opened Château La Coste in Aix-en-Provence several years ago, all of which use open flames to cook.

You don't need to cross the Channel (or the Atlantic) to try his traditional Patagonian fire cooking, however. Here, Mr Mallman reveals his five tips for the perfect flame-grilled steak.

CHOOSE THE RIGHT MEAT

To make good food, you first need good produce. To do that, you need some information about the animal and you also need to use your eyes. Then you need to get a good cut. I prefer a ribeye. The best type comes from bigger animals. If you ask for steak from a one-tonne cow, it will have better marbling in the meat. Those lines of fat through the meat mean a better flavour. Next thing to find out is if the meat has been aged. And I don't mean dry aged. I prefer meat that has been hung up in a cold room for 21 days in its whole form. You get a better flavour if the animal isn't broken up until it has been hanging for that amount of time.

2

GET THE RIGHT WOOD

It is important to get really good-quality wood. It must be dry and it must also be a type that produces very hard charcoal. The wood will vary depending on where you are in the world – in Argentina, quebracho or algarrobo; in the US, mesquite; in Europe, certain oaks work. The reason why this is so important is because cooking over flames requires a relatively stable heat for a relatively long time. Put simply, you need stuff that will give you red embers that last long enough to cook properly for a long time. On flames, you also need a steady heat. This is incredibly important or your meat won't cook evenly.

3

KNOW YOUR TIMINGS

I never use a meat thermometer. I know young chefs do and I understand why, but, to me, it is better to go with instinct and eyes. Timing is always very important in cooking, but it is all the more important when you are cooking on flames. You can't simply put the meat on the flames for an hour and just pop back a couple of times to check it. You need to have an idea of the heat and how long it is going to be before your meat is overcooked. It is essential to know when to withdraw the meat from the fire. You want to get that nice crust on the meat, so you want the wood hot, and you don't want to mess with it, or you will damage the crust. The question is, how do you know when to do that? By experience. There is no way to know until you try it yourself. I could write a book about this subject, but it wouldn't be as useful as figuring it out for yourself.

4
CONCENTRATION IS KEY

You have to be constantly observing when you are cooking with fire. You have to have the concentration and, of course, you need patience. Patience is a very potent thing. What I do involves fires that burn for 16 to 18 hours. We start at maybe 1.00am the night before we will serve our food. My chefs will be constantly moving around looking at the flames. Though I allow myself a comfortable chair and lots of coffee, I will still be staring at the fire, trying to read what is happening with the wind. Is it moving the fire around? Is it making it hotter? You are looking at the potential of the embers. You are looking at how it is sizzling. Is the meat contracting because of too much heat? One surefire sign that your meat is medium is when the side furthest from the flames seems to bleed. To me, if it is bleeding, then it is a sign that it has been overcooked.

5
YOU NEED GOOD COMPANY

Cooking this way can take a long time, and who wants to spend hours cooking alone? So get a glass of wine and someone to talk to. I am absolutely convinced that if you have good company and are in good spirits, the food will end up more delicious. This is a gaucho [Argentine cowboy] custom, to some extent. I say to some extent because they can also be very silent men. If you join four of them for lunch, they will tell some jokes or play guitar for a while, but then they can become very silent. They enjoy silence and are used to it, but that doesn't mean you have to.

THE BEST PIZZA ON THE PLANET

From Berlin to Brooklyn, the world's finest slices outside Naples (and just outside Naples)

PIZZERIA POPOLARE *Paris*

Paris may boast many great things, but it's rarely a cheap place to eat good Italian food. Pizza Popolare, as the name suggests, has heard the people sing and offers Neapolitan pie at Neapolitan prices. What's more – because this is France – despite the imported Italian ingredients, there's no need to bow to Italian dough diktats. Based in the second arrondissement, Popolare is one of a run of sharp yet modestly priced trattorias in the capital from the rapidly expanding Big Mamma Group.

What to order
Trial the monthly rotating truffle special, such as the Truffle Burrata Fiction, which mixes creamy burrata with Parisian mushrooms, grilled courgettes, fresh truffles and a *crème de truffe noire*.

111 rue Réaumur, 75002 Paris. bigmammagroup.com

STANDARD *Berlin*

"Serious pizza" exclaims Standard's logo, a useful counter to the suggestion that *pizzaiolo* Mr Alessandro Leonardi's food is as run-of-

The Double Truffle pizza at Pizzeria Popolare, Paris

the-mill as its name implies. Located in a bourgeois neighbourhood on the outskirts of Mitte, Austrian Mr Florian Schramm opened this pizzeria in 2014. The tomato sauce is made from tomatoes fresh from the volcanic soil of Mount Vesuvius – you don't get much more Italian – and the pies made by Mr Leonardi, a graduate of the Academy of Naples' official Association of Pizza Makers, are known as the best in the city.

What to order
Standard does do the Naples thing – the margherita and a marinara dominate the menu, alongside pizzas topped with imported Italian ingredients such as pecorino and *capocollo* – but also offers white pizzas boasting smoked cheese and cured meats. *Das gute Zeug.*

Templiner Straße 7, 10119 Berlin. standard-berlin.de

ROBERTA'S *New York*

Before it became known as New York's buzziest pizza joint – you may have seen Marnie eating there in season two of *Girls* – it would be easy to miss Roberta's now-famous red door. On the outside, chef Mr Carlo Mirarchi's restaurant looks innocuous enough, but inside it's a sprawling wonder with a giant Italian-import, wood-fired pizza oven and a radio station. Mr Mirarchi offers a full menu, which has grown around the pizza, led by delectable vegetable-based dishes – think summer beans with fresh ricotta and roasted shisitos with cashew mostarda.

What to order
Roberta's is a complex restaurant disguised as a dive bar. It does simple very well. Order the 12in margherita and delight in a product with the moist centre of a Neapolitan pie and the stiff crust of a New York pizza. Match it with one of the 14 orange wines (who knew?).

261 Moore Street, Brooklyn NY 11206. robertaspizza.com

PEPE IN GRANI *Caiazzo*

Va' fa Napoli! Or rather go to Caiazzo, just north of the ancient city, where Mr Franco Pepe sources all the ingredients from within a few kilometres of his restaurant. He ferments his dough for 72 to 96 hours (much longer than most) and the result is a stunning pie that has repeatedly secured

Pepe In Grani the accolade of best pizzeria in Italy (and most popular nominee in pizza bible *Where To Eat Pizza*). For those reasons, get there early (think UK dinner time) to beat the queues. Mr Pepe makes 500 pizzas a day – by hand, no less – and once they're gone, they're gone.

What to order
Mr Pepe is no stickler for topping purity. His menu features ingredients from fig preserve to anchovies. In the spirit of minor invention, try his margherita *sbagliata* (margherita made wrong), a spread of tomato purée and basil reduction on a mozzarella-topped dough.

Vicolo San Giovanni Battista, 81013 Caiazzo. pepeingrani.it

PIZZA STUDIO TAMAKI *Tokyo*

In 2012, Mr David Chang (of Momofuku-empire fame) caused some consternation among pizza purists by declaring the planet's finest pie was to be found in Japan – at Seirinkan ("House of Holy Wood"), where genius *pizzaiolo* Mr Susumu Kanikuma has been serving impeccable margheritas and marinaras for 25 years. Pizza Studio owner Mr Tsubasa Tamaki is one of a host of Kakinuma disciples devoted to evolving the Tokyo-Neapolitan style – distinctive for delicate dough with a seared crust, cooked in a locally crafted oven over Japanese wood.

What to order
Cooked at nigh on impossible-to-wrangle heat, Tamaki's (cheeseless) marinara is sublime. Fancy a more complex creation? Opt for the Bismarck – mozzarella, mushrooms, pecorino romano, homemade sausage and Benikujaku egg.

1 Chome-24-6 Higashiazabu, Minato City, Tokyo 106-0044

BÆST *Copenhagen*

You don't need to be fluent in Danish to translate the name of chef Mr Christian Puglisi's stylish Nørrebro eatery. He may make the finest pizza dough in Copenhagen, but at Bæst, the beast is king. Charcuterie is made in-house from some of Denmark's finest swine and served alongside homemade cheese, both of which make it onto Bæst's short, but glorious, pizza menu, which features a mixture of local and Italian flours.

What to order

Mr Puglisi is an alumnus of Noma, the restaurant that has redefined Danish cuisine. Which means that while margheritas are on the menu, you can see the influence of Noma's founder, Mr René Redzepi, in some dishes, too, notably Pizza No.6, which is cooked with Bæst's own take on soft Puglian stracciatella cheese and topped with oyster mushrooms and nettles. But no live ants as yet.

Guldbergsgade 29, 2200 Copenhagen. baest.dk

BRÁZ PIZZERIA *São Paulo*

São Paulo takes its pizza as seriously as anywhere outside Italy, even New York. Thanks to the city's huge population of Italian descendants, there are five times as many "Italians" here as there are in Naples. An annual pizza day, celebrated on 10 July, gives you a hint of its popularity. Sunday is the big family pizza day in São Paulo, where its 6,000 neighbourhood pizzerias are ambushed by hungry Brazilian families, hankering after the huge thin-crusted pies to be found in joints such as Bráz, which, across its seven locations, will serve thousands of pizzas from its wood burners.

What to order

Pizza Bráz. Brazilians have put their own twist on their adopted dish – think corn and creamy Catupiry cheese. The house special is simple but effective. Fernandinho rather than Neymar Jr. It's covered with sliced courgette, garlic and olives, and topped with mozzarella and parmesan.

Various locations, São Paulo. brazpizzeria.com

Opposite page: Tomato, Bæst mozzarella and basil pizza at Bæst, Copenhagen

HOW TO MASTER THE FINE ART OF DAY DRINKING

A guide to enjoying cocktails in the sun without ending up in the gutter

Words by Mr Samuel Muston

On summer afternoons, usually around 4.00pm, I think of Saint Augustine of Hippo. Or his prayer, at least: "Please God, make me good, but not just yet." It is the lament of the day-drinking man. Let the day roll onwards and brighter still, but stop me from sliding off my seat like an eiderdown in the night (thanks, Ms Nancy Mitford, for that). Therein lies the trick: how to go far, but not too far.

Drunkenness is a condition to which we are all entitled. Not all of the time or you become a bore (or dead). No one wants to be like Mr Evelyn Waugh – he might have been the greatest English novelist of the 20th century, but he got in his cups too often in the afternoon. In her memoir, the Duchess of Devonshire (the youngest Mitford sister) described him as "tricky company" due to the "phenomenal amount of drink the writer downed... You had to catch him early in the evening. He was full of compliments, but they turned to insults before you knew where you were."

It is a knife-edge battle, which is best won with a nibble of food – not so much that you sink in somnolence, but enough that you don't call your host a toad. An Aperol spritz is sensible; a Campari and soda wise. A large plate of carbohydrates is better still.

But you must be careful not to tip over that gossamer edge. Even if the person you are drinking with is as forgiving as Queen Mary, who, hosting a three-sheets-to-the-wind 1st Earl of Birkenhead (then a judge) on the Royal Yacht, watched as he vomited on the table, and coolly said, "I'm sorry to see that lobster does not agree with the Lord Chancellor". For his part, he later asked, "Should I be drunk as a lord or sober as a judge?"

Drinking in the sun, you feel like the bee that has acquired the florist. In part because you are not supposed to be doing it. In the day, you are supposed to be doing something productive. Striving. Earning. The thing to do is form a little party of afternoon expeditionary. The more of you, the greater the transgressive pleasure.

Choose your drinking partners carefully. You don't want a Hegelian philosopher, but nor do you want someone like the writer Mr Simon Raven. He disappeared on his wife on so many afternoons that the arrangement became permanent. She did once track him down and sent him a telegram saying: "Wife and baby starving send money soonest", to which he replied, "Sorry no money suggest eat baby". You want frivolity, not wholesale abandon. Mr Raven spent his final years in an almshouse "for distressed gentlemen", having drunk away the proceeds of his life's work. A big chunk of it between 12.00pm and 5.00pm, no doubt.

Enjoy your day, but know when to retreat. Remember: you can only get away with being disgustingly drunk if you are very good-looking or under 25. And drink some water too, will you?

WHAT TOP CHEFS EAT AT HOME

From tacos to a mulberry tart, even culinary wizards crave comfort food. Follow their recipes below and tuck in

Words by Mr Adam Coghlan

Critically acclaimed restaurants are often characterised by food that, if not always "fine", is technically accomplished. Food that, by design, is difficult to recreate at home, the product of talented chefs who have been rigorously trained and have access to the best available ingredients. And yet chefs are people, too, who want to make the most of their free time and eat food that is satisfying, sustaining and easy to prepare, but no less delicious than what emerges from their restaurant kitchens. From one-time Noma head chef Mr Matt Orlando's carne asada tacos to Italian master Mr Massimo Bottura's peasant passatelli, here are six recipes the world's most exciting chefs turn to for comfort.

CARNE ASADA TACOS WITH SALSA FRESCA, GUACAMOLE AND CREMA *(previous page)*

Mr Matt Orlando, owner and head chef, Amass, Copenhagen
Tacos remind Mr Matt Orlando of home. "I grew up 15 minutes from Mexico, so I have a special place in my heart for Mexican food," he says. It was a cuisine he grew up eating and cooking, especially at "age 15, working in a kitchen in which the cooks were all Mexican". These days, he gets to eat carne asada about once a year, straight from the airport, at La Posta De Acapulco, his favourite taqueria in San Diego.

Ingredients (serves 4)

For the tacos
1.4kg (3lb 1oz) flank steak
3 Corona beers (or other Mexican-style beer, eg, Pacífico)
Bunch of coriander, coarsely chopped
2 onions, thinly sliced
Juice of 5 limes
4 jalapeños, sliced into rings
3 tbsp salt, plus extra to taste
Corn tortillas, to serve

For the salsa fresca
6 tomatoes, diced
1 red onion, finely diced
Juice of 2 limes
1 jalapeño, finely chopped
Half a bunch of coriander, roughly chopped

For the guacamole
4 ripe avocados
Juice of 2 limes
Quarter of a bunch of coriander, roughly chopped

For the crema
1 part drained yoghurt
2 parts crème fraîche
A splash of beer

Method

Take the taco ingredients, except for the steak, and mix until the salt is dissolved. Place the steak in a leak-proof bag or bowl, cover with the marinade and leave for 12 hours or overnight. Remove the meat from the marinade and pat dry.

Prepare a grill (preferably over hot coals) or heat a heavy-bottomed griddle pan and grill the meat until medium, about 2 minutes each side. Let the meat rest for 15 minutes before serving, then slice thinly across the grain.

Season with additional salt if necessary. Serve with corn tortillas, salsa fresca, guacamole and crema.

For the salsa fresca, about 30 minutes before serving, combine all the ingredients in a bowl. Season to taste.

To make the guacamole, pit the avocados and spoon the flesh into a mixing bowl. Place the rest of the ingredients in the bowl and mash roughly with the back of a fork. Season to taste.

SUGAR ROSEMARY BUNS

Ms Elena Reygadas, chef and owner, Rossetta, Mexico City
"I am a fervent bread consumer. I'm passionate about it," says Ms Elena Reygadas. Its warming, versatile qualities lend it a particular suitability to the cold season. "This is a crusty and very comforting bread you can eat at any time of day," she says. Its style – sweet, salty and fatty – comes as much from the lard breads of Britain as it does from Mexico.

Ingredients (makes 24 buns)

1.2kg (10 cups) flour
1 ½ tbsp salt
14g (1 ½ tbsp) dry yeast
300g (1½ cups) lard
300g (1½ cups) sugar
Handful of rosemary sprigs, leaves picked and chopped

Method

Mix the flour, salt and yeast with 800ml (3½ cups) water to form a dough. Knead, allow to settle for 10 minutes, then roll out and smear the lard, mixed with the sugar and rosemary, across the surface of the dough to form a glaze. Cut into 24 squares and fold each four times. Place on a greased baking tray and allow to ferment for 45 minutes.

Preheat oven to 230°C (450°F). Bake for 20 minutes, then turn the oven up to 250°C (500°F) for a further 10 minutes. The aim is to get the buns golden brown, but if they begin to brown early, cover with foil for the final 10 minutes.

SPELT WITH ROASTED CABBAGE AND PRAWNS

Mr Ben Greeno, head chef, Merivale, Sydney
"I love this because it reminds me of holidays," says Mr Ben Greeno of his recently invented "fridge raid" supper. "I discovered it a year ago, coming home from work one night with a few ingredients. I threw it together and finished it off with some amazing seaweed butter made by Jean-Yves Bordier, which we'd brought back from France."

Ingredients (serves 4)

Half a white cabbage, cut in half
300g (1¾ cups) spelt
70g (1 cup) grated parmesan
100g (½ cup) seaweed butter (or blend 100g butter with 3 sheets of dried nori and 1 tbsp salted kombu)
120g (4¼ oz) cooked prawns
1 lemon
Salt and pepper

Method

Preheat oven to 180°C (350°F). Roast the cabbage in a pan on the stove until black on the sides, then transfer to the oven and cook for 25 minutes. Cover the spelt in 4cm (1½ in) water and boil until tender, about 20 minutes. Drain, but don't cool down. Reserve any remaining cooking water.

Chop the cabbage into chunks and add to the spelt. Return to the pan and add the grated parmesan, seaweed butter and prawns. Mix together until the cheese and butter have melted and emulsified.

Loosen with a little spelt cooking water or stock. Add a squeeze of lemon and season to taste.

MULBERRY TART

Mr Dave Pynt, owner and head chef, Burnt Ends SG, Singapore
"Mulberries are a sign that summer is coming in Australia – the excitement of the holidays and Christmas," says Mr Dave Pynt. "They have a very sweet, but slightly acidic rich berry flavour." He feels nostalgic about this dish, too. "We always had a mulberry tree in our garden growing up, so I've been around them from a very young age," he says. "Although mulberries are always best straight from the tree, one of my favourite ways to serve them is on top of this tart with honeyed Chantilly cream."

Ingredients (serves 8)

For the tart base
100g (½ cup) butter
60g (½ cup) icing sugar
20g (1½ tbsp) almond flour
Pinch of salt
1 egg, beaten
165g (1½ cups) plain flour

For the tart filling
240g (1¼ cups) unsalted butter
240g (1¼ cups) caster sugar
240g (2 cups) almond flour
3 eggs, beaten
Large handful of mulberries,
to finish
Honeyed Chantilly cream,
to serve

Method

To make the base, mix the butter, icing sugar, almond flour and salt together until soft and fluffy. Add half the egg until emulsified, then add the rest. Add the flour until it is only just incorporated – don't over-mix it. Tip onto a lightly floured work surface, and roll out into a sheet 3mm (⅛ in) thick. Refrigerate for 45 minutes. Blind-bake in a lined tart tray for 40 minutes at 150°C (300°F). Remove from the oven and leave to cool.

To make the filling, beat the butter and sugar until smooth. Add the almond flour and then slowly incorporate the eggs. Make sure it is well-combined. Pipe the filling evenly into the base and bake in the oven at 150°C (300°F) for 40 minutes. At 35 minutes in, just before the end, remove the tart and sprinkle the mulberries across the top. Return to the oven for the remaining 5 minutes. Serve with honeyed Chantilly cream.

NONNA ANCELLA'S PASSATELLI

This classic Modenese countryside dish, taken from the *cucina povera* (poor kitchen) tradition of frugal home cooking, is Mr Massimo Bottura's grandmother's recipe, which she taught the would-be chef when he was five. It's "a flavour I grew up with", says Mr Bottura. On chilly Sundays around a table with his family, Mr Bottura reminisces about his mother and grandmother, "the women who brought me into the kitchen and showed me that cooking is an act of love".

Ingredients (serves 4)

150g (2½ cups fresh; 1 cup dry) breadcrumbs
100g (1½ cups) grated parmigiano reggiano
Pinch of ground nutmeg
Pinch of lemon zest
1 litre (2 pts) chicken stock
3 eggs, beaten

Method

Place the breadcrumbs, parmigano reggiano, nutmeg and lemon zest in a shallow bowl. In the meantime, bring the stock to the boil. Add the eggs to the dry ingredients. Mix together in a uniform ball of dough.

Place the dough in a ricer and press it directly into the boiling stock. Cook the passatelli until they surface, about a minute. Serve hot with the stock in a bowl.

How to:

DRESS FOR FANCY RESTAURANTS

The notion of a "fancy restaurant" is itself a little antiquated. The spots with the toughest tables in the world – Noma, Pujol, The French Laundry – won't give a toss if you're in a T-shirt or a tuxedo. With that said, occasion dining remains a concern, and for some of us a pleasure. Whether it's a special date night or an important client dinner, there are still plenty of times when you'll want to look your best, or at least appropriate. Here's what to know.

THE GROUND RULES

Live for the moment

These days, few restaurants would turn you away for violating a dress code. But when choosing an outfit for dinner, you're pandering to the occasion, not the establishment. Is it a birthday? Then, you should make the effort. Catching up with friends? Jeans and a T-shirt is fine. Read the situation properly and you should never feel over- or under-dressed.

Turn it down a notch

A basic, but essential piece of advice: if you're eating, dress in dark colours. Not only are they easier on the eyes post-sunset, they make it far easier to get away with any spillages. If you're desperate to add a bit of colour, turn to your accessories – a watch with a deep-blue face, or a patterned pocket square can make all the difference in candlelight.

Go easy on the cologne

Dining is a sensory occasion – and we don't just mean what you put in your mouth. In fact, 80 per cent of the sensation of taste is down to smell, so beware of spraying too much fragrance. Take special care around wine enthusiasts: they will *not* appreciate your patchouli while they're trying to discern subtle notes of gooseberry in their sauvignon blanc.

Freshen up

This nugget of advice is aimed at the bearded gentlemen of the world, though it's not going to hurt the rest of us. Simply: wash your face, before and after eating. The unfortunate truth is that facial hair attracts lingering odours and fragments of food, which, as they grow more elderly, also grow more... oh, do we have to spell it out? Just do it, OK?

Keep it loose

The whole point of dinner is putting things into your body, and when that happens, your body expands. So, it's safe to say you should avoid that slim-fit cotton-elastane Prada shirt you bought in the 1990s and can still *just about* squeeze into. Opt for garments that fit comfortably, knowing that, at some point, you might want to loosen your belt a notch or two.

THE DETAILS

The blazer

When it comes to dinner, this is your workhorse and your saviour, a quick way to look just smart enough that can also be easily discarded should the moment call for it. Black is perhaps a little too formal for most occasions – and is often worn by the waiters – so if you're looking for a safe choice, we would recommend navy or dark grey.

The shirt

The benefit of a shirt at dinner is that it allows you to wear a pattern without sacrificing conviviality or formality. And, like dark colours, patterns are good at hiding accidents. For non-wedding dinner purposes, we recommend a variety in a dense madras or micro-check, worn with the top button undone.

The trousers

Should you wear jeans to dinner? Well, if you like. But we would advise leaning towards a smarter variety, that is, in raw, unwashed denim, not yet worn enough to be faded. An even better option? Wool trousers – sharper, sleeker, and much more dinner-appropriate for establishments at the fancier end of the spectrum.

The shoes

In a restaurant, your feet are generally under the table, so there's no point worrying about this part too much. Go for something smart yet functional, such as a pair of Derby shoes, or, if you prefer sneakers, plain leather tennis shoes. Avoid statement sneakers – there's a time and place, of course, we're just not entirely sure it's at the dinner table.

The wallet

We'll leave it up to you to work out who pays – though we would say it's always nice to offer, if you can. But for the purposes of making the whole process as elegant as possible, avoid bringing your workaday, bulging billfold wallet with you to dinner. Instead, opt for a slimline, elegant cardholder, which will fit easily in your blazer pocket.

7

MEET THE MEN MAKING FASHION MORE FRIENDLY

We all need someone to talk to. With that in mind, we asked a few friends in the fashion industry to explain what bonds them together

Words by Mr Chris Elvidge

In 2019, we launched MR PORTER Health In Mind, a campaign designed to help men lead healthier and happier lives. And here, we take a look at one of the foundational pillars of a fulfilling existence – friendship.

What is it, exactly, that makes a good friend? Why are we drawn to certain people rather than others? And what are the benefits of comradeship in the workplace? Rather than try to explain it ourselves, we decided to ask a few people from the realm of menswear to share the details of their closest and most enduring friendships.

Fashion isn't exactly known as the friendliest of industries. Indeed, it's often perceived as cut-throat, insular and highly competitive. In an environment such as this, friendships are more important than ever.

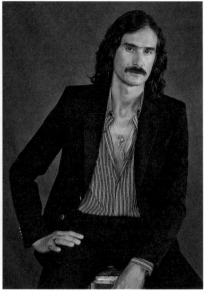

MR LUKE DAY *fashion director, GQ UK*
AND MR BEN COBB *editor-in-chief, Another Man*

You don't have to spend long on the menswear scene to cross paths with Messrs Luke Day and Ben Cobb. They are two of the industry's most colourful characters. Neither of them can zero in on the precise moment they met. Mr Cobb hazards a guess that it was at a Giorgio Armani show about 15 years ago. They've been inseparable ever since and have accompanied each other through many of life's big moments. "Marriages, divorces and funerals," says Mr Day. "We've done it all."

What were your first impressions of each other?
Mr Cobb: I remember thinking that you seemed shy, which I found interesting. Because you had quite a look on.
Mr Day: That makes sense as I'm quite protective around new people. I'm going to have to be honest and say I can't actually remember meeting you.
Mr Cobb: Well, that says a lot.

What do you like about each other?
Mr Cobb: Luke's very open once he knows you and feels comfortable. He doesn't hide how he feels – it's all out there.
Mr Day: I'm very present in my emotions. And I need a lot of emotional support. So, I'm lucky to have friends I can turn to, like Ben.
Mr Cobb: I think it's quite amazing and it's made me open up more, too.

Mr Day: Ben has the call to adventure – this free-roaming, Sagittarian thing. Whereas I would naturally err on the side of caution. And I like that about him. He helps me step outside of my comfort zone, because I suppose I feel safe with him.

In theory, shouldn't you be professional rivals?
Mr Cobb: People do say that, but I've never had that feeling at all. When something great happens to one of us, we both have cause for celebration.
Mr Day: And it's not as if we're really competing with one another, anyway, because we have such different points of view.

It's refreshing to hear you both speak so openly about one another.
Mr Day: Well, maybe that's true. But I love how things are changing. It shouldn't be a shameful thing to show vulnerability. Or to be kind. And now that it's seen as the right thing to do, it feels like we can all finally relax. Because it's the easiest thing to do, too. It's what comes naturally.

MR MATTHEW BREEN *founder, Devaux*
AND MR TOMMY TON *creative director, Deveaux*

Messrs Matthew Breen and Tommy Ton first crossed paths in New York City while the former was running Carson Street Clothiers. He later went on to launch the luxury menswear brand Deveaux, and when it expanded into womenswear in 2018, Mr Ton joined the team as creative director. The two men share an outsider status of sorts, Mr Breen having come to fashion from the law, while Mr Ton first made his name as a street-style photographer for gq.com and style.com.

What do you remember about your initial meeting?
Mr Ton: The New York menswear scene was an interesting place back then because it felt like at one moment it was non-existent and the next it was everywhere. All of these guys were suddenly fanboying over fashion, which I thought was hilarious.
Mr Breen: He enjoys making fun of me about that to this day.
Mr Ton: There was this little clique of guys who were really interested in fashion despite coming from a background that had nothing to do with it. It was fun to become friends with them because they saw me in a different way from how I saw myself, which was nice. I'm very shy and I struggle to see myself as anything more than someone just doing their job.
Mr Breen: The first time I met Tommy, he was like a celebrity, at least in the fashion scene. Our little crew was super intimidated by him, not

realising that he was actually quite a shy guy. But once everyone figured each other out, it was the beginning of a good friendship.

Mr Ton, you've moved on from photography, but back in the day you were the guy, right?
Mr Ton: I wouldn't say I was "the guy".
Mr Breen: You were 100 per cent the guy.
Mr Ton: I think I just had a big platform, working with the publications that I did at the time. People knew that if I took their photograph, there was a good chance that it would make it onto gq.com.
Mr Breen: There definitely came a point when Tommy was getting followed around by street-style wannabes, but it wasn't always that way. The first time I saw him, I thought, this dude works really hard. It'd be 95°F in Florence and he'd be sprinting around, playing *Frogger* with cars to get the right shot. He was the only guy doing that.

How has it been, Mr Ton, going from photography to fashion design? Do you feel at home?
Mr Ton: Yes and no. I still think of myself as something of an outsider. I've found my own family in this industry, but I'm still greatly intimidated by certain aspects of it.
Mr Breen: I'm also an outsider in the industry, coming from the law, but my perspective is a little different from Tommy's. The menswear side I've found to be quite congenial for the most part.

MR JERRY LORENZO *founder, Fear of God*
AND MR KERBY JEAN-RAYMOND *founder, Pyer Moss*

Mr Jerry Lorenzo and Mr Kerby Jean-Raymond run two of the most exciting labels to have emerged from the US in recent years. They first connected in 2018 after Mr Lorenzo saw Mr Jean-Raymond's work on Instagram. A few months later, Mr Jean-Raymond requested that Mr Lorenzo interview him for one of Hypebeast's digital-only cover stories. They spoke about sneaker collaborations, spirituality and their experiences as men of colour in the fashion industry, all themes that continue to bind them together.

You're on different sides of the country. When do you find time to meet?
Mr Jean-Raymond: We gravitate to one another when we're in the same city. When I was in Los Angeles, we hung out, went to Complexcon. Now we're here [in Paris], I'm dragging him out at night.
Mr Lorenzo: It's hard. I'm an old man now. I'm a dad.
Mr Jean-Raymond: For real, though, one of the things I respect most about Jerry is that he's a family man. Seeing someone in my industry who has reached a level of success that I aspire to, but who also has a functional relationship and a family life – that gives me hope, because it's something I never saw when I was growing up.

So his success has provided a roadmap for your own?
Mr Jean-Raymond: For sure. When he and I first met, my career was

in a completely different place. His career took off sooner, so I had the chance to watch him walking around with security, all these kids running towards him. Now that's kind of like what I'm going through. But had I not seen how he handled it with grace, I probably would have folded.

Mr Lorenzo: I like to offer Kerby as much as possible. Now I have a chance to pour into someone who I really believe in, it's like a giving well. You give to it, and it gives back to you.

So, you think it's important to have an ally when you're coming from a place of marginalisation?
Mr Lorenzo: A thousand per cent. Kerby came into my life at a time when, I didn't realise it, but I needed someone that I could lean on. And I think that, with Kerby, our friendship wasn't ever really about the fashion. It's about the brotherhood.

Mr Jean-Raymond: It's the same way for me. The fashion is the thing that we do, but who we are is what connects us.

MESSRS SINAN ABI AND PER FREDRIKSON
co-founders, Séfr

Messrs Per Fredrikson and Sinan Abi met on the football pitch in their early teens. They formed an immediate bond and have done almost everything together since, from taking their first trips abroad without parents to spending four months backpacking in Southeast Asia. In their twenties, they set up a small vintage store in Malmö called Séfr, or "zero" in Lebanese Arabic. It has since blossomed into a menswear brand.

What were your original impressions of each other?
Mr Fredrikson: I remember Sinan walking towards the football pitch with this tough-guy look on his face. My first impression couldn't have been more wrong because he's the friendliest, most sociable guy I know.
Mr Abi: He always tells this story. I was really focused that day, that's all.

Is it fair to say you saw something in one another?
Mr Abi: We definitely felt an interest for each other, a kinship. We wouldn't have met if it wasn't for football – we were from completely different neighbourhoods in Gothenburg.
Mr Fredrikson: But after that, we did everything together. School classes, holidays, starting the business...

It must have felt like you were taking a big risk with the business.

Do you think either of you would have done it alone?
Mr Abi: It's not risk that would have put me off doing it alone. I just don't think it would have been as much fun without Per.
Mr Fredrikson: It wouldn't have been the same without someone to share it with. And it's comforting to know that you have someone by your side when things go wrong, too.

Does this also help you as colleagues?
Mr Fredrikson: For sure. In the beginning, we did everything together. But as we've got used to each other's skills and characteristics, we've divided the work up a lot more. And because we trust each other completely, we're comfortable doing that.
Mr Abi: Also, I get the feeling that people like to hang out at our office. It feels like a welcoming place. It's got a nice, relaxed vibe. And that's because our relationship is built on a solid foundation of mutual respect.

You both have young children. How has this affected your friendship?
Mr Fredrikson: I actually changed Sinan's oldest's nappy just yesterday.
Mr Abi: For me, meeting Per's son, when I see him, I feel some connection to him. I don't know how to explain it. Maybe it's because of the love I have for Per. My fiancée always says that the relationship I have with Per is really beautiful, and that I should feel very grateful for having that. Because we accept each other 100 per cent, for everything we do.

HOW TO APPEAR WISE

From ordering wine to taunting classic car owners, upgrade your cultural cache with this handy cheat sheet

Words by Mr Dan Davies

There are few things worse than the sensation, mid-conversation, of a trapdoor opening beneath your feet as you're suddenly confronted with the murky waters of your own ignorance. Yes, in this digital world, we are better informed than ever, such is the speed and ease with which we can access information. But it's often difficult to discern, out of all those crucially important things you ingest via Buzzfeed and Reddit, which bits of cognitive flotsam will keep you afloat in that most terrifying of environments: real life. For here, unfortunately, you're likely to find yourself face-to-face with a wide variety of sentient, unbookmarkable humanoids, some of whom you might be keen to impress. There are many potential pitfalls – social scenarios where you need to find something intelligent to say, but don't have time to think for a few minutes before clicking "send".

How to muddle through? It's been said that a little knowledge goes a long way, although Socrates perhaps put it better: "To know is to know that you know nothing. That is the meaning of true knowledge." We'll call that lesson one. With this in mind, we've put together the following guide to appearing intelligent, cultured, well-educated and captivatingly opinionated. Good luck!

ORDERING WINE AT A RESTAURANT

You find yourself at a top-class restaurant with company you are trying to impress. There is no logical reason for taking charge of ordering for the table. But you do, and now you must deliver.

Luckily, help is at hand in the form of the sommelier – you will appear most wise by seeking him out and listening to his advice. A good sommelier will expect to be told, however quietly, the purpose of your visit and how much you wish to spend, and advise accordingly.

Mr Nicolas Clerc, brand ambassador at Armit Wines, *Decanter* World Wine Awards judge and previously master sommelier at Fields, Morris & Verdin, suggests that if, even after enlisting a sommelier, you still feel the need to broadcast your wine knowledge, you should try asking what he has discovered recently or which vintages are showing well. Then, if the prices are still a bit steep, suggest the sommelier recommend "something more convivial and easy" – he'll get the message.

Do say

"I normally order champagne to start, white burgundy for the starter and a red bordeaux for the main course, but tonight I'm feeling adventurous, so I'm going to listen to your suggestions."
(My mouth might be saying these words but look into my eyes – they are pleading for your help.)

"I hear that Germany and Austria have some spectacular dry whites right now, but what I'm really interested in are the gastronomic-style reds coming out of Spain and Italy. Do you have any?"
(I'm grandstanding, humour me.)

Don't say

"We'll take the second on the menu."
(I'm cheap, but don't want to look it. Exploit my embarrassment by selling me something at the highest profit margin possible.)

"Give us the most expensive wine you have."
(I am clearly an idiot.)

AT A CONTEMPORARY ART GALLERY

You're in a typical white-cube gallery space surrounded by champagne-quaffing, loafer-wearing contemporary art cognoscenti. You're alone and standing before a neatly arranged pile of dust that has been topped with a hammer, sundry nuts and bolts, and a half-eaten ice cream cone. Suddenly, you become aware of a presence at your shoulder. And then, the dreaded question: "What do you think?"

Fear not, for your would-be interrogator has committed one of the cardinal sins of the private view: asking for an opinion. There are no right and wrong answers in contemporary art, so avoid being drawn onto hazardous terrain by nodding repeatedly and issuing the get-out-of-jail-free response: "It raises a lot of questions." Having demonstrated that you are comfortable with the "challenging nature of the project", you can then walk on.

"An engagement with why a work might be hard to penetrate is a completely valid part of the aesthetic discussion," advises Mr Luigi Mazzoleni, director of the Mazzoleni art gallery in London, which specialises in post-war Italian art. "Too much attention can give you away as an amateur as much as too little, so the tempered approach is best."

Do say

"The piece works well within the space."
(I don't know what I'm looking at, but I used the word "space" instead of "room", so I have a right to be here.)

"I'm intrigued by the artist's visual lexicon."
(I like the colours.)

"Has this work been shown publicly before?"
(I might not look like one, but can you be sure I'm not a serious collector?)

Don't say

"How much is that one?"
(I've had enough free champagne and it's time to go.)

"My four-year-old could have done that."
(I'm a hopeless case.)

IN A MEETING

Instead of following the presentation on next year's action points, you've been checking Instagram. So, when asked for an opinion, make like you've been attending to an important work-related message and then swing into action.

Economist Ms Sylvia Ann Hewlett, author of *Executive Presence: The Missing Link Between Merit And Success*, argues that how you act (gravitas), what you say (communication) and how you dress (appearance) are the keys to winning the respect of your bosses.

In other words, it's all about impression management. In the boardroom, it's likely you're in the company of creative, charismatic or dominant personalities, who, research suggests, are more adept at deception (and identifying it). Most likely, you already know how to make a good impression via your dress sense. But how do you bounce back from the "my bad" with the phone?

The first step is be convincing. Avoid non-verbal leakage. Don't touch your mouth, neck or throat, or shuffle your feet – they're all giveaways that you're mentally spinning. Verbal "tells" include repetition, offering too much "padding". Try to stay calm. Grace under fire is a key element of "executive presence", so establish eye contact, build empathy and deftly pass the ball back by saying something vague yet direct, such as "Do all the stakeholders have buy-in?" Then, most importantly, turn your phone off and switch on.

Do say

"It's great, but is it scalable?"
(I don't really know what the word means, but I appear ambitious yet cautious, and it's someone else's turn to talk now.)

"How will it play out across social media?"
(I may know nothing about this, but I bet you know nothing about Instagram.)

"I'd like to do a deeper dive on some of the implications and report back."
(Give me a couple of days and I'll come up with a decent response.)

Don't say

"Sorry, I zoned out for a second."
(I know we all make mistakes, but I'm too dumb to realise no one ever admits to them.)

"I agree completely."
(If anything goes wrong, you can now blame me.)

AT A CLASSIC CAR SHOW

Although you appreciate classic cars, your knowledge of their mechanics and provenance is cursory. But that doesn't stop you from starting an ill-advised conversation with the owner of a vintage two-seater racing car at the Goodwood Festival of Speed. Why do you do these things to yourself, eh?

The object of his devotion, you have been breathlessly informed, is a 1954 Ferrari 375-Plus Spider Competizione, with a 4.9-litre V12 engine mounted in the front. Now is not the time to comment on its lack of coffee-cup holder and parking sensors, but to ask the right questions. "Are all the parts original?" would be a good start, followed by enquiries about whether the car is still driven or for Concours d'Elégance events only.

Finish up with some general cooing over the coach-building brilliance of legendary car designer Mr Battista Pininfarina and walk away... slowly.

Do say

"The earliest variants are always the best. It's the car in its purest form. Just look at the E-type Jaguar or Lamborghini Countach."
(My home, like yours, is filled with beautiful, undriveable old bangers.)

"The real opportunity for collectors is in 1980s icons such as the BMW 5 Series or the Porsche 964."
(The market at the top end has peaked. Sucker!)

"I'm not sure matching numbers really mean that much any more."
(I have a working knowledge of a hot topic in classic car collecting, specifically that not all components in cars have numbers that match the VIN [vehicle identification number] on the chassis.)

Don't say

"Can I take it for a spin?"
(I've thoroughly misunderstood this classic car thing.)

"Not very reliable, are they?"
(My car never breaks down. But I do, often. In fact, I might cry right now.)

AT A DINNER PARTY

As the dessert plates are cleared and the cheese board arrives, conversation turns to philosophy. Your university (or high school) exam notes are a distant blur (especially since the host brought out the port), so what are you going to say to the earnest-looking chap to your left with the big questions?

British philosopher Mr AC Grayling might have insisted on reading literary works in the morning and philosophy in the evening, but your busy schedule (aka iPhone addiction) means your attention is occasionally diverted away from actual literature. Your first piece of armour is the knowledge that people who talk about philosophy are not philosophers.

"Ask questions, listen to the answers and take them further, if you can," advises author Ms Marianne Talbot, a director of studies in philosophy at the University of Oxford. "The more you listen to the other person, the wiser you'll seem to that other person. In philosophy, we discuss arguments in accordance with the principle of charity. This tells us that the person we are arguing with is sensible and rational, that he loves truth as much as we do."

But what if this guy is intent on parading his knowledge, and your lack of it? "Try Karl Popper," says Ms Talbot. "He said no theorist can ever claim to know something positive. At best, we can know that something isn't true when our attempts to falsify it have succeeded."

Do say

"Was Professor Stephen Hawking right to have said that philosophy is dead because philosophers don't pay enough attention to science?"
(I see your philosophy and I raise you quantum physics.)

"Does modern philosophy have anything to say to today's moral dilemmas? For example… [something topical]."
(You may have read Kant, but I've read the internet.)

Don't say

"A priori", "A posteriori", etc.
(I'm going to try and evade you with fancy words. Please take me down.)

"Wise men say only fools rush in."
(I'm just a really big Elvis fan. Will that do?)

A GUIDE TO SOUNDSCAPING YOUR PARTY

Let Hollywood music supervisor Mr Randall Poster show you how to take an evening from cool cocktailing to burning down the house

Words by Mr Randall Poster

We've all been to that party where two glasses of punch transform the mild-mannered host into a one-man Sugar Hill Gang. In the best case, Bacchic dancing ensues. In the worst, he will only relinquish his iPhone (which he insists on referring to as "my wheels of steel") after the guests have left. No one wants to be *that guy*, do they? We don't want you to be *that guy*.

So, we asked Mr Randall Poster – who has worked with Messrs Wes Anderson, Martin Scorsese, Sam Mendes, Richard Linklater, Harmony Korine, Todd Haynes, Todd Phillips and more – for some tried and true techniques for creating a chill-and-chat cocktail hour that gradually builds into an Ibiza-worthy rave. Plus, a few party-enders to send the guests home (when you want) with smiles on their faces.

So, without further ado, here is Mr Poster's well-worn blueprint for a night to remember.

1 EASE ON DOWN THE ROAD

At the start of a party, it's key to let your guests settle into things. Your musical selections will set the stage. Let them know that they are in the right place at the right time. Play to personal (and the evening's) aspirations. Acknowledge Mr Miles Davis. People will begin to lean into the evening and start to savour the surroundings. You will find yourself thinking of the word *décolletage*. Ms Billie Holiday fell in love with Mr Ben Webster, and when you play "La Rosita" by the jazz legend, everyone else will, too. But be careful that the music doesn't intrude on the simple social conventions of introduction and basic greetings. Bossa nova is not to be underestimated.

2 HAPPY TOGETHER

Familiarity breeds contentment, so remember to play some ready favourites. You want to hear someone say, "Oh, I love this song!" within 45 minutes of commencing. Refill all flutes and glasses. Perhaps a sweet reminder of the miracle of Mr Marvin Gaye; the permanent genius of Mr Joe Strummer; that sweet soul of Ms Chaka Khan. These songs return us to our younger selves, other parties and other moments in time. And here we are together. An anthropological dig of another sort – this is where Mr Rod Stewart meets Mr Sylvester Stewart meets Mr Jermaine Stewart.

3

IT'S MY PARTY

Mr Vince Guaraldi's "Linus & Lucy" into The (English) Beat's "Stand Down Margaret" into "Once In A Lifetime" by Talking Heads. Your party has officially peaked. This has been a magic trifecta for me over the years and has inspired multiple generations of rug-cutters from the basements of Providence, Rhode Island, to the hallways of the Covent Garden Hotel and beyond. There is tempo and there are polyrhythmics. There is sweet spirit and there are spirits. Those not rendered speechless will thank you for this.

4

MYSTERY TRAIN

On the flipside, drop something new and rare. Give the people something they don't yet know they love. Find fulfilment knowing you've helped sell a few albums. This is where you cast your vote for the Mercury Prize. Where you pay homage to Messrs Anthony Gonzalez and Chilly Gonzales. Perhaps the moment to share your secret obsessions: Perfume Genius. Jarami.

5

LET'S DANCE

I've never felt that it's truly a party unless you get some people to shimmy and shake it. Don't be afraid to start. The secret is in the beat. Try some American hip-hop from 2 Live Crew, electronica by Boys Noize or *that* song by Robyn. This is the most precious part of the evening – when thought is sidelined and the kinetic reigns. Think Mr Kanye West, or "When You Were Mine" by Prince.

6

LOVE ON A TWO-WAY STREET

Now it's time to take the pulse of the party. Look around. Are people having enough of a good time? Have I mentioned my love for Ms Lily Allen? Have you played anything from the latest Jungle record? Try a bit of Drake, Rihanna or Future. And finally, and only if they've earned it, drop "Get Me Home" by Ms Foxy Brown. No explanation necessary.

FIVE COMMON MISTAKES

SURRENDERING THE DECKS
Nearly everyone admires their own taste in music. They will want to share. Stand guard. Smile. Say no. Be calm and carry on.

HOUSE PARTY, NOT A RAVE
A touch of trap. A taste of trance. All fun fare, but remember your friends are drinking wine, beer and spirits, not cradled in a cerebral vortex of ecstasy (seemingly). Thus, they will need certain dramatic musical momentum to keep things moving in the right direction. Avoid the extended dance remix.

HOOTIE & THE BLOWFISH
Never. Ever.

"TOMMY, CAN YOU HEAR ME?"
Keep an eye and ear on the crowd. Too much volume can spoil the chance for conversational connection, but meek music mutes magic. Mine the fine line. But drop it like it's hot.

MR KNOW-IT-ALL
Let people know what they're listening to, but don't be a bore. You're throwing a party, not teaching a class. Parties are for fun, not for lessons.

CONTRASTING COMPANIONS

The world would be a boring place
if we all dressed just like our mates.
Here we celebrate a handful of our
favourite odd couples

Words by Mr John Brodie

MR RICHARD AVEDON *photographer*
AND MR FRED ASTAIRE *dancer, singer and actor*

What man wouldn't want Mr Fred Astaire to play him in a film? In *Funny Face*, a musical set inside the fashion world, Mr Astaire plays a photographer named Dick Avery, loosely based on Mr Richard Avedon, who acted as a technical adviser on the film. Mr Avedon always dressed classically, despite growing up in Manhattan as the child of two parents in the fashion industry. Here, he is pictured in a Brooks Brothers button-down, a crew-neck sweater and a mackintosh. Mr Astaire, who patronised Anderson & Sheppard, Hawes & Curtis, and would "get lost for days in the Burlington Arcade", was a master of looking casual in well-made clothing. His trilby hat is the perfect touch of sartorial sunshine on a rainy day.

Opposite page: Messrs Richard Avedon and Fred Astaire on the set of *Funny Face*, The Tuileries Garedens, Paris, 1957

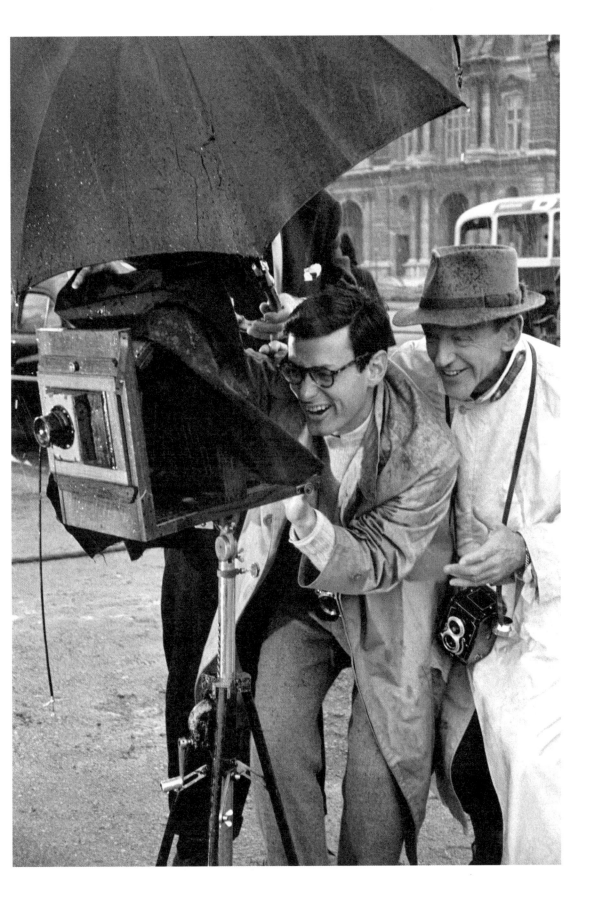

248

MR DAVID HOCKNEY *artist*
AND MR WILLIAM S BURROUGHS *writer*

One dresses for sun; the other for rain. When the British artist Mr David
Hockney did a series of lithographs of the American writer Mr William S
Burroughs in 1981, he was creating sun-drenched masterpieces from his
house-cum-studio in Los Angeles' Nichols Canyon. During those years,
his dress was that of a perennial schoolboy, putting a technicolour and
cheeky spin on the classics – as he does to add some flair to his suit
when the two reunite in the above image taken at the Naropa Institute
in Boulder, Colorado, in 1989. Mr Burroughs' harrowing accounts of
addiction included *Junky* and *Naked Lunch*, yet he dressed conservatively.
While many of his fellow Beat Generation writers preferred workwear,
Mr Burroughs looked no different than any other Harvard man – except
perhaps for his hard-boiled fedora.

Messrs David Hockney and William S Burroughs in Boulder, Colorado, 1989

249

MR ANDY WARHOL *artist*
AND MR MUHAMMAD ALI *boxer*

The image was taken in 1977 at Mr Muhammad Ali's training facility in
Deer Lake, Pennsylvania, where the boxer was preparing for his fight
against Mr Earnie Shavers. Mr Andy Warhol, who was working on his
Athletes series, was not a natural sports fan, but he was fascinated by
the loyal following athletes commanded. "His problem is he's in show
business," he said of Mr Ali to the author Mr Victor Bockris, who had
accompanied him that day and took the above image. "I'm surprised
fighters don't take drugs, because it's just like being a rock star. You get
out there and you're entertaining 30,000 people." The two provide a
beautiful contrast in styles. Mr Ali was fresh off a two-week European
tour wearing black from head to toe. Mr Warhol delivers a bit of preppy
summertime perfection in a seersucker Oxford-cloth shirt and a repp tie.

Mr Andy Warhol and Mr Muhammad Ali (with Ms Hana Ali) in Deer Lake,
Pennsylvania, 1977

SIR WINSTON CHURCHILL *former UK prime minister*
AND MR ARISTOTLE ONASSIS *shipping magnate*

Even though Sir Winston would become a frequent guest on Mr Onassis's yacht, the *Christina O*, the friends approached dressing from different mindsets – the British politician and the continental tycoon. As a young man serving under Lord Horatio Herbert Kitchener in the Sudan, Sir Winston had worn the uniform of the 21st Lancers, and as an elder statesman, he still dressed formally, even in balmy climes. Meanwhile, Mr Onassis wore the suitings of a boulevardier or terry-cloth polos, swim shorts and espadrilles. So even when the occasion called for both to be dressed up, theirs was a Continental vs British play-off.

Sir Winston Churchill, Ms Athina Onassis, Lady Clementine Churchill and
Mr Aristotle Onassis in Istanbul, 1950

MR ALBERT EINSTEIN *physicist*
AND SIR CHARLIE CHAPLIN *filmmaker and actor*

While on a 1931 tour of the US, Mr Albert Einstein, who was still a German citizen at this time, was introduced to Sir Charlie Chaplin during a tour of Universal Studios. The two developed an immediate rapport. "What I admire most about your art is the universality," Mr Einstein said to Sir Charlie. "You do not say a word, and yet... the world understands you." To wit, Sir Charlie replied, "But your fame is even greater. The world admires you, when nobody understands you." Sir Charlie invited Mr Einstein to be his guest at the premiere of his film, *City Lights*, a few evenings later, where they show their varying approaches to black tie.

Mr Albert Einstein and Sir Charlie Chaplin attending the premiere of *City Lights*, Los Angeles, 1931

252

MR JACK NICHOLSON *actor*
AND MR GROUCHO MARX *comedian*

By 1972, Mr Groucho Marx was divorced for the third time and living in Beverly Hills. He, like many in the entertainment business, felt very staunchly against the war in Vietnam and was a supporter of the Democratic presidential candidate Mr George McGovern. In his later years, he had dropped some elements of his on-screen persona (the tailcoat with necktie) in favour of a look more suited to a French philosopher at Les Deux Magots: a beret and a blazer worn over a crew-neck sweater. Like Mr Marx, Mr Nicholson enjoyed a good cigar, but on style they part company – Mr Jack Nicholson is seen here in white overalls and a multicoloured short-sleeved shirt.

Messrs Jack Nicholson and Groucho Marx at a party for Mr George McGovern, Los Angeles, 1972

MR JOE DIMAGGIO *baseball player*
AND MR FRANK SINATRA *singer*

The most celebrated baseball player and the most popular singer of their
generation had much in common. Both were the children of Italian-
American immigrants, and both were married, then jilted, by luscious
starlets – Ms Marilyn Monroe and Ms Ava Gardner, respectively. Still,
their friendship was complicated. In this image from March 1949, the
relationship is new. Mr DiMaggio is at the beginning of what would be
a championship season and wears the classic pinstripe uniform of the
New York Yankees. Off the field, Mr DiMaggio dressed conservatively
and all-American. This is perhaps a subconscious reaction to the fact
that his parents, along with thousands of other Italian, German and
Japanese Americans, were classified as "enemy aliens" by the government
after the bombing of Pearl Harbour. Mr Sinatra felt no such need for
understatement, appearing here in a double-breasted peak lapel suit.

Messrs Joe DiMaggio and Frank Sinatra at Yankee Stadium, New York, 1949

HOW TO CHARM FOLLOWERS AND DAZZLE INFLUENCERS

A man-about-town's guide to making your personal brand shine

Words by Mr Raven Smith

For the amateurs among us, a party is a vehicle for fun with free-flowing booze and the potential to meet someone more attractive than your ex. The truth is, a party is merely the backdrop for an extended theatrical presentation. It demands professionalism.

Your personality and the unique alchemy of your tastes are the aces in your self-marketing deck. And any (good) party is an invaluable opportunity to extend your reach. What you choose to transmit at such events needs to add colour and intrigue. Personal brands are a form of self-mythology, but, like Joseph's amazing technicolour dreamcoat, you draw attention while hiding the real you. The objective is simple: growth of following. A party provides ample access to potential devotees, like wild steeds ready to be lassoed into your belief system. Saddle up.

MAKE AN ENTRANCE

There's no point sashaying into an empty room. Always be an hour late. Never apologise. Shine bright like a diamond and showcase that proverbial razzle-dazzle. Wear something to catch the eye – something shimmering or sheer. Electric boots. A mohair suit.

INTRODUCTIONS MATTER

Maximise every initial interaction. Grip that hand a little too tight, maintain eye contact a beat too long. Project the aloof-yet-familiar quality specific to the top boys at school who didn't know you existed.

FAKE IT TILL YOU MAKE IT

Mention a country pile or summering in Deià and the jet set will flock towards you. Much like the horses they ride, grooming and breeding are pillars of the rich. Evoke total nonchalance, or full-tilt glamour.

PERFECT SMALL TALK

Any human would rather bite into a scented candle than listen to an anecdote about your dream, so be the Rocky of banter and keep the small talk punchy. Painful though it might prove, there could be an introverted gem secreted amid the sheeple. At least one full chat circuit is essential.

BE ENTICING

It was easier to charm the socks off people before iPhones gave them the attention span of a gnat. Lightly tickle your audience with short Christmas-cracker jokes and easily digestible fortune-cookie wisdom.

KNOW HOW TO SELF-PROMOTE

To slay at self-promotion, you have to foam-finger your brilliance like a Warriors fan at an NBA final, while simultaneously projecting Mr James Dean-level cool. When sharing salacious intel regarding your latest triumph, make it apparent you're too important to even be there.

LEAVE A LEGACY

We all wish our fellow man would drown in the reservoir of our personality, bask in our depths and depart for ever changed by the interaction. Crop-spray guests with pure charisma.

BE EVERYWHERE, ONLINE AND IRL

Social media and physically socialising are late capitalism's yin and yang. And both are key. After an intensive night of wooing fresh minions with enigmatic flair, you need to be bracingly confessional online, sharing the minutest details of your "life".

HAVE THE BREAKDOWN OFF-STAGE

Finally, all of this (net)working is to eternally remain behind the scenes. Sweating, fretting and existential questioning must be internalised. Save the meltdowns for your therapy sessions.

BONUS: BE READY TO DO IT ALL AGAIN

A rigorous post-party skincare regimen should iron out all your wrinkles. The city never sleeps, but you need to look like you get eight to 10 hours a night, so bulk-buy those moist stickettes for eye bags.

How to:

DRESS FOR A PARTY

The first rule of parties is that you should dress up. From lounge suit to black tie, there are many ways to make sure you're putting your best foot forward. Of course, not every party needs a tuxedo – we're looking at you, pub birthdays – and there are always rules, spoken and unspoken to adhere to (ignore the dress code at your peril). But once you've worked out the level of pizazz your fête requires, there are few pleasures greater than delivering it. Here's how to get it right.

THE GROUND RULES

Read the invitation

A strong start to any party is knowing exactly where it is and at what time. But reading the invitation with care is also important to make sure you're au fait with the dress code so you don't turn up in a smart-casual look to a black-tie event. If it's unclear, ask.

Indulge yourself

The worst offence you can commit is not turning up to a party. The second is to arrive determined to be no fun. Get in the mood by wearing something special. An eye-catching detail, patterned shirt, dazzling watch or a sharp suit all say you've made an effort.

Plan to let loose

Planned fun might seem like a misnomer, but you're not exactly going to have a great time if you haven't thought this through. If dancing is involved, you should be prepared to take off your jacket. In that inevitability, make sure what's underneath is not an embarrassment.

Come prepared

Parties need charmers, so be one of them by turning up with a stash of things people might need. Include party must-have items such as paracetamol or a lighter, and a handkerchief for anyone who needs a shoulder to cry on.

Choose the right fragrance

Parties require us to celebrate each other's company, even when we get immensely sweaty. Counteract eau de merriment by embracing strong fragrance – something intense from Frederic Malle or TOM FORD – and wear lots of it. The key notes to look for here are wood, leather and musk.

THE DETAILS

The hair

In the rush to pull off a sartorial winner during party season, your hair can often feel like an afterthought. Book an appointment with your barber ahead of the big night and invest in a good gloss-finish pomade. This will make your hair really pop in photos.

The dinner jacket

Party dress codes shouldn't be broken, but they can be played with. Even a black-tie event leaves some wiggle room. A velvet dinner jacket adds a splash of fun, while a midnight-blue evening suit is also a winner in the night-time stakes.

The shirt

In this department, white is the obvious choice, though if your dinner jacket is navy, a light pink can also be nice. If you're wearing a bow tie, pick a shirt with a bib front, which will create a surface of pristine white. Anything more, such as ruffles, is strictly for the showstoppers.

The cufflinks

Don't clown around with these. For cufflinks, pick an accent colour that chimes with your jacket. Keep it simple – gold, silver, pearl and onyx are great options. For further guidance, your metals should agree with any watch or shirt studs you might be wearing. No novelty allowed.

The watch

"What time is it? Party time!" Make sure you leave the dad lines at home, but do wear a dress watch if you really want to win at the biggest social occasions. Keep it classic, preferably gold, with a suitably stylish alligator or a polished-leather strap.

8

THE PERFECT HOME IS WHAT YOU MAKE OF IT

Why every stage of life has
its own wallpaper

Words by Mr Jeremy Langmead

In 53 years, I've lived in 24 different houses — an average of less than two-and-a-half years per home. That's a lot of decorative schemes and paint charts. An entire warehouse of furniture. To begin with, my mum moved a lot. By the time I turned 18, we'd gone through nine properties. It wasn't so much that she got bored of where she lived; she got bored of whom she lived with. She cast aside husbands like King Henry VIII did his wives: divorced, died, detained, divorced, survived. So packing up my belongings then rearranging them again somewhere else (with someone new) was how I grew up. I learnt from the very best.

My mother was an expert at extracting herself from a place of co-habitation. When she left her fourth husband, only six months into their marriage, I remember standing in their kitchen, watching as she methodically took what was hers from the cupboards while her broken, sobbing husband looked on in disbelief. "Tony, were these wooden spoons yours or mine?" she would ask in a tone that suggested she was doing nothing more dramatic than the morning's crossword. Eventually, a transient way of life becomes the norm — until it slowly dawns on you that you're a kind of traveller, just a little more Renault Mégane than Romany.

Once I reached my early twenties, I craved a home of my own. After such an unsettling upbringing — plus eight years of sharing dormitories with 23 other boys at school — I wanted stability. I longed for somewhere where I couldn't hear my mother bickering with a husband; somewhere with a wardrobe that an alcoholic stepfather couldn't hide his empty bottles of booze in; somewhere I could display my incongruous collection of Ms Beatrix Potter china figurines and back issues of *The Face*. So, when I got my first job, fresh out of university and with a salary of £11,000 per annum, I immediately started hunting for a flat of my own.

But with my meagre pay packet, nothing was within reach. Reluctantly, I teamed up with an old school friend, Stephane, to purchase somewhere together. Before too long, we found a light and airy, if somewhat shabby, flat in north London for £79,000. We put down a deposit of £1,000 each, miraculously got a mortgage agreed and it was ours. Aged 23, we were homeowners. It was only then that I realised that years of domestic trauma had turned me into a decor dictator. Poor Stephane barely had a say in how the flat would look. I allowed him to choose the colour of his bedroom walls and the kitchen, which I would barely use.

I spent the next few months bidding for furniture at the Criterion auction house on Essex Road, painted the sitting room and hallway Imperial Chinese Yellow, and went for a Moroccan theme in my bedroom. Every time Stephane tried to introduce something of his own to our shared living space, I would promptly dispatch it to his bedroom. We reached an impasse with a ginormous rubber plant that he insisted should live in the sitting room. I hated it. Its 1970s vibe did not go with my cut-price Sibyl Colefax & John Fowler scheme. Each morning, after Stephane left for work, I would pour household bleach into the plant pot. But it stubbornly refused to die. And its continued existence saddened me on a daily basis.

A few months later, in another effort at conjuring the domestic bliss that had eluded me as a child, I bought a kitten. Stephane tolerated the litter tray halfway up the staircase, forgave the playful mayhem the kitten caused when left alone during the day and didn't mind playing with it each night while I was out at various nightclubs. What Stephane didn't realise was that he was merely nurturing his tree's future assassin. Well, assassin's aide. After a few weeks, when the kitten was a fraction bigger, I hatched an evil, but, frankly, genius plan. I waited for Stephane to depart for work, then pushed the rubber plant over, snapped the trunk in two and left it for dead. That evening, I feigned surprise as Stephane told me of the grotty crime scene that had greeted him. "Oh no," I sympathised. "That pesky kitten. I can't believe he did that." Stephane obviously couldn't quite believe it either. "I don't understand how its falling onto the carpet would have caused the trunk to snap," he puzzled.

Eighteen months later, I moved out to live with my girlfriend. Once we were married, I sold my half of the flat to Stephane. Due to a recession and my minimal equity, all I got for it was £800. I spent the entire sum on a Prada leather jacket. Stephane bought lots of new plants.

Moving in with a partner is another rite of passage in one's interiors life. You have to find a style that you both like and learn to compromise. You need to kindle passions for decorative schemes that you can readily share and afford and, within time – in our case, a scant six months – adapt to take into consideration the needs of a baby. Sisal becomes impractical, coffee-table tableaux unwise and storage for mounds of ugly plastic toys a top priority. For this next stage, I cast aside my aristocrat-falls-on-hard-times approach for something clean and contemporary. My mother-in-law was married to Lord Norman Foster and so we were greatly influenced by the amazing, triple-height, riverside Battersea penthouse they lived in, and subsequently tried to apply his steel-and-glass aesthetic to our diminutive three-bedroom Victorian terrace nearby.

During your twenties and thirties, your approach to interiors is heavily guided by budget (hello, Ikea) and a plethora of TV shows and magazines (or now websites), as well as a gritty determination not to have a home that resembles your parents'. What you need from a residence can quickly change with relationship status, parenthood and even jobs.

When, in my late thirties, I became the editor of *Wallpaper** magazine, a publication that championed Italian furniture, Scandinavian minimalism and Brazilian architecture, my quirky Hackney house with

its bright pink walls and perky mishmash of furniture and paintings no longer seemed appropriate. Since I was now divorced and my sons lived with their mum, I sold up and bought a loft in Shoreditch. It was huge and open plan. You could cycle around the living space, buy giant pieces of furniture that looked like they'd been crafted by Nasa and stare out onto the grisly-sounding hen parties spilling out into the streets below.

At first, there was something freeing about starting all over again, not having any clutter and living directly above one of the capital's most fashionable restaurants. But after a year, I began to realise that it wasn't really me. I was now 40 – that joyous stage when you truly care much less about what everyone else thinks. So, off I went, once again.

Next came a charming garden flat on a magical square in Primrose Hill. It hadn't been touched in decades. There were dead animals behind the radiators, 20-year-old meals adhered to the kitchen surfaces and a smell of cabbage emanating from the drains. None of that put me off. The style I went for was bisexual Bloomsbury artist meets 1970s playboy. I bought first editions of all nine of Mr David Hicks' interiors books and tried to imitate his knack for mixing old and new, colour and pattern. There were dark, ornate wallpapers, brown Carrera marbles, low lighting and objects and paintings galore. I realised the look had worked when one night a famous young actor asked if he could use my flat as a shag pad while I was away. (The answer was no.)

Another few years, another marriage – another move. We needed space, fresh air, a bigger garden, no neighbours... More rooms to decorate. As your life becomes more hectic, your work more time-consuming and your time left on Earth palpably shorter, a sense of escape and tranquillity becomes more desirable. You yearn for a nest, a refuge where no one asks anything of you.

Still, in the nine years I've worked at MR PORTER, I have moved three times. And I am about to do so once more. My shrink and I often discuss why I'm forever looking for the next place. With each new home, I'm intent on creating a domestic utopia. When it (inevitably) doesn't quite make the grade, I pack up and try again. Ultimately, I don't think I truly want to find perfection. It's the journey I enjoy. I like the distraction of buying stuff, creating Pinterest boards, dreaming up a fresh stage set for the next chapter of my life. Despite fighting it since childhood, I'm more like my mum than I care to admit.

So where am I now? Mr Charles and Ms Ray Eames, two of the most influential furniture designers of the 20th century, had it right. Despite their strong design aesthetic, they believed that your home should tell your story, that shelves should host an eclectic collection of objects that you've accrued over the years. You should be able to cast your eyes around you and be reminded of a life well travelled and, ideally, one well lived. Fortunately, now that we've all become more design savvy, thanks in large part to the internet, we are confident enough to be more eclectic in our tastes. Ikea now sells chintz, for example. *Wallpaper** magazine now celebrates maximalism as well as minimalism.

Most important of all is to accept that your home has to function for the life you lead now, rather than the one that you hope to lead one day. What you need and want changes all the time. And that's as it should be.

One of my sons, who recently graduated from university, has just moved into a flat-share in east London. He proudly showed me around. His bedroom was cramped and overlooked a supermarket car park.

"It really is perfect, Dad," he said. "I wake up in bed and all I can see is my collection of sneakers."

"It's a shame about the view," I said, looking out at the Tesco Metro.

"What do you mean?" he replied. "I can get up, look out and all I see is where to buy my cigarettes. Doesn't get better than that."

Meanwhile, I'm moving to Cumbria. I'm buying a small farmhouse in the land of lakes, mountains and Mr William Wordsworth. The house is surrounded by wild flowers with far-reaching views across green, fertile valleys. The Lake District is where Ms Beatrix Potter wrote her books. My china figurines of Mrs Tiggy-Winkle and Jemima Puddle-Duck are finally coming home.

NINE PRO TIPS FOR PRIME INTERIOR DECOR

From clever lighting to investing in art, here's how to furnish your home with style

Words by Ms Susannah Butter

Designer Mr Ed Ng and architect Mr Terence Ngan have a flair for creating spaces that pack a punch. Over the past two decades, the Hong Kong-based duo behind AB Concept have transformed restaurants and hotels the world over, cutting a high-design dash across most of the world's great cities. Their trick, if you can call it that, is to adopt "a narrative-driven approach" that "fuses traditional and modern elements" or, in other words, bringing together old and new and giving their constructions a sense of place. They have been wildly successful at it, too. Name a city and you will probably find an AB Concept bit of design there. From the Yun House restaurant at the Four Seasons Hotel in Kuala Lumpur to the former Central Police Station in Hong Kong via the W Hotel in the Algarve, Portugal, they are past masters of their art. MR PORTER asked Mr Ng for nine tips on decorating your home in a stylish way.

BUY ART

Art is the one thing you should always invest in. It is what will spark joy in your home, to borrow a phrase from the Japanese tidying guru Ms Marie Kondo. The right painting or sculpture provides a centrepiece for a room. Just let the art shine. The last time I went to Lisbon, I picked up a large piece of sculpture for my mountain home in the woods of Karuizawa in Japan. It is made of timber and has a hole in the middle, I placed it by the window to frame and accentuate the view. I feel like the timber is living a new life there.

LIGHT UP

There is no such thing as too many lights. Clever lighting is essential in making a home. LED bulbs make the light warmer and deeper than traditional tungsten and create a better atmosphere. Mid-century lights contrast well with modern sofas. I buy my lights from vintage shops. Mirrors can also enhance light and shade. They can be used in two ways, decoratively or architecturally. They essentially serve as an extension of perception of space and must be placed strategically. Use them to borrow the natural light and project it into darker areas. Take care not to overexpose areas that should remain dark by design.

VINTAGE IS YOUR FRIEND

Vintage shops are wonderful and ensure that your house will look distinctive with one-off pieces that no one else has. But always make sure you take a moment to consider carefully whether you should take something home before you buy it. Can you see it in your house? Inspiration is everywhere. In a Milan villa I discovered a valet cabinet. In the old days, you put your laundry in one side and servants took it out the other, cleaned it and then put it back on your side. It was made for elegant living.

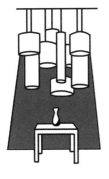

FIND A FOCAL POINT

Pick one thing you love and
develop your space from there.
It can be an antique fireplace or
a work of art. If you centre on
that, the rest can be minimal.
I like walls to be neutral so that
everything else stands out. Off-
white and shades of grey work
wonderfully with my art.

TAILOR THE SPACE

Think about how you will use the
rooms. We had a banker client who
gets up at 6.00am, so in addition
to the master en suite, we built a
bathroom inside a wardrobe so
he didn't disturb his wife in the
mornings. If you want to entertain,
consider that experience. You may
want spaces to mingle. Maybe you
want a beautiful garden pavilion
or a beautiful weathered oak table
to sit around. Plan how you want
spaces to be used.

SPEAK TO
THE LOCATION

Play to the strengths of your
surroundings. For instance,
my house in Milan is decorated
with Italian antiques, inspired
by the old villas I love there.
My favourite room is the living
room in my Japanese mountain
house in Karuizawa. The whole
building is designed around the
view and the fact that, when you
arrive, you can smell the cedars.

EVOLVE

A home is a living object. Don't
be scared to add and take away
from it, rebuilding if necessary.
It will evolve with you, and tastes
will change. Move with that.
I work very fast. If I see something
I like, I will want it immediately,
but sometimes I make mistakes,
so I force myself to go back later
and tweak things.

BREAK RULES

I don't generally follow trends.
I have noticed that there has
been a clean, minimalist trend
for many years, but now that is
changing. People are appreciating
the artisanal movement and using
more eclectic designs. One client
used 10 types of fabric in her living
room and it had such an impact.
It's like you can't go wrong if you
just cook a beef steak in oil, but
adding ingredients can make it
distinctive. Your home offers a
similar chance to aim higher and
dare to express yourself. That gives
you the wow factor.

EVERYTHING IN MODERATION

Don't over-furnish. It is better
to have a slightly emptier space
to start with than for it to look
too full and clumsy. Do justice to
every piece you buy. If you love
an object, it shouldn't be put in
the corner. In our restaurants
and hotels, it is important to tell a
story, to impress and engage. It's
different for homes. They're about
you and what you like.

THE 10 DESIGN CLASSICS EVERY MAN NEEDS IN HIS HOME

Timeless furniture and homeware guaranteed to impress armchair critics

Words by Mr Tom Morris

PULCINA COFFEE POT (*opposite*) BY MR MICHELE DE LUCCHI, ALESSI

You've heard the one about an Englishman, an Irishman and a Scotsman walking into a bar, but have you heard what happened when an Italian coffee maker, designer and manufacturer walked into a café? The Pulcina coffee pot was designed by Mr Michele de Lucchi, one of the founding members of the Memphis Group, in 2015. He collaborated with the coffee roaster Illy and utensils maker Alessi on research into what would make the ultimate coffee pot. Pulcina's spherical shape means air can be put under pressure before it boils to improve flavour. Its beak-like spout avoids drips, and it looks fantastic. Finally, something to give the beloved Bialetti espresso maker a run for its money.

TEA TROLLEY 901
BY MR ALVAR AALTO, ARTEK

No home is complete without a decent selection of spirits for when you have guests. And for that, nothing tops the 901 tea trolley (don't be fooled by the name; it's perfect as a small bar), created by Finnish design master and architect Mr Alvar Aalto for the Paris World Fair in 1937. Mr Aalto and his wife, Ms Aino Aalto, travelled widely and were inspired by the tea-drinking cultures of Britain and Japan when it came to designing this trolley. The 901 is made very simply. It comprises two loops of laminate held together by shelves and sits perfectly somewhere in the middle of elegance and charm.

LAMINO CHAIR AND FOOTSTOOL *(opposite)*
BY MR YNGVE EKSTRÖM, SWEDESE

There is something unquestionably "granny" about easy chairs with wooden arms, especially given the bed-like cocoons that are so popular among sofa buyers today. Yet drink one cup of coffee sitting in the Lamino chair with your feet resting on the accompanying footstool and you will never look back. It is an ergonomically faultless and fluffily fantastic gem of a sheepskin chair. Designed in 1956 by Mr Yngve Ekström, one of the leading lights of Swedish modernism, the Lamino has won numerous design awards and has never gone out of production. "To have designed one good chair might not be a bad life's work," said Mr Ekström. Indeed.

BROWN BETTY TEAPOT
BY MR IAN MCINTYRE, CAULDON CERAMICS

There are few words more likely to inspire a shudder in design fans than "reissue". All too often this means a "modern take on an old classic" that essentially means shinier packaging, a heftier price tag and questionable provenance. Not so with Queen Victoria's favourite teapot, the Brown Betty, when it was given a proper going-over by ceramicist Mr Ian McIntyre. Making it fit for purpose for decades to come, Mr McIntyre inverted the concave lid so the pot could more easily be stacked in cupboards, turned the spout to make it non-drip and added an infuser for those who like tea made from leaves. The illustrious 2018 Betty has been made marginally more thoughtful via this clever reinvention.

SYSTEM CADO
BY MR POUL CADOVIUS

Decent shelving is seldom thrilling, but get it right and you will be eternally rewarded. There are few better options than the eminently smart Cado system designed by Danish master Mr Poul Cadovius in 1960. Faced with smaller homes in cities, Mr Cadovius hit upon the idea of getting everything – tables, desks, book shelves, cabinets – off the floor and onto the wall. Other designers and manufacturers had the same idea in the post-war period, but whereas many of those creations were made of metal and somehow felt more appropriate for an office, the warm and "woodsome" Cado system was ideal for the domestic environment.

ORIGINAL 1227 DESK LAMP
BY ANGLEPOISE

Few bedsides, desks or living rooms wouldn't be improved with the addition of the 1227 lamp, created by British manufacturer Anglepoise in 1935. It is the archetypal light and peerlessly practical. In 1932, the automotive engineer Mr George Carwardine turned his expertise to lighting and developed a design for a task light that could be moved and held in place using special springs. He approached his pals at Herbert Terry & Sons to make the 1227 lamp, and they soon registered the Anglepoise brand. In the years after, the light was adapted for use in hospitals and military planes. Its ability to shine light just about anywhere it is pointed explains why the 1227 lamp remains a bestseller the world over.

ODEON CUTLERY *(opposite)*
BY MR DAVID MELLOR

Mr David Mellor was born in Sheffield in 1930 and studied at the Royal College of Art during the early 1950s, something of a golden age of British design. His generation, which included Sir Kenneth Grange, Ms Margaret Calvert and Sir Terence Conran, were encouraged and expected to design across various different sectors. Mr Mellor, who died in 2009, designed a postbox, bus shelter and the UK traffic-light system (still used today), but he is perhaps best known for his cutlery. He created tableware for use in British embassies, hospitals and prisons (commissioned by the Government) for decades, but it is his flat, spare, minimal Odeon collection that remains his most iconic.

620 SOFA
BY MR DIETER RAMS, VITSŒ

In his renowned *Ten Principles For Good Design* written in the 1970s, German industrial designer Mr Dieter Rams didn't have a great deal to say on the importance of flexibility. And yet that is what makes his 620 chair programme, designed for British manufacturer Vitsœ in 1962, such a roaring success. The chair is sold in modular units, which can be added to over time. An armchair in your first flat in your twenties can easily become a loveseat in your thirties and then a whole three-seater by the time you have upgraded to a bigger house. It remains an iconic piece of design more than half a century after it was conceived.

S285 DESK AND S64 CHAIR *(opposite)*
BY MR MARCEL BREUER, THONET

Last year marked the centenary of the founding of the Bauhaus design school, a collective located in Weimar, Germany, that included founder Mr Walter Gropius, textile artist Ms Anni Albers and teacher Mr Mies van der Rohe. Bauhaus design was known for merging art with technology. and the S285 desk and S64 chair – formed of rock-solid tubular steel frames paired with wooden supports and designed by member Mr Marcel Breuer – are excellent manifestos for the principles developed by the school 100 years ago. Whether or not Mr Breuer envisaged the reliance we would one day have on decent domestic workspaces is debatable, but this set-up is perennially perfect for work-from-home days.

HIROSHIMA CHAIR
BY MR NAOTO FUKASAWA, MARUNI

It takes a lot for a new chair to come along and challenge the all-star favourites such as the perennially chic Wishbone by Mr Hans Wegner or the supremely comfortable Eames fibreglass design. But in 2008, thanks to Mr Naoto Fukasawa, one of Japan's finest living industrial designers and the man behind the wall-mounted Muji CD player, a new icon was born. Made in Japan, the Hiroshima chair has a cradling slope, which means it is perfect both at a dining table and behind a desk. It is minimal, timeless and pared back in that emphatically 1960s way and, available in beech or oak, which will develop a wonderful patina over time. Truly, it's an investment piece, as every good dining chair should be.

FIVE EASY WAYS TO USE LESS PLASTIC

Disposable packaging, bags
and bottles are killing the planet,
here's what you can do to stop it

Words by Mr Sam Fishwick

It's difficult to live in the 21st century and not contribute to the plastic problem. About 8,000,000 tonnes of the stuff pours into the oceans each year, and by 2025, there will be enough to cover five per cent of the world's surface in cling film. We're literally sealing the planet's fate.

In the past few years, the reputation of single-use plastics has turned to trash. After all, it takes several lifetimes to break down. Call it *Blue Planet* politics, but the sight of an albatross trying to feed her chicks with plastic precipitated a sea change in attitude towards polymer waste.

And the tide has been turning. As of 2019, some 127 countries introduced complete or specific bag bans and levies, or were in the process of doing so. This year, a ban on straws, stirrers, and cotton buds comes into force in England, while the EU has adopted a plan to cull a longer list of items by 2021. But the 78 million tonnes of packaging produced yearly won't disappear overnight. Here are five ways to redress the balance.

REUSE, NOT REFUSE

Turning down single-use plastics is only a first step. We all need to own our own reusables. Ms Sarah Booth, a sustainability blogger who has previously lived plastic free for a month, takes a reusable coffee cup, steel water bottle and cutlery set with her everywhere. "The fact they're reusable saves energy and prevents plastic pollution and I love having quirky, brightly coloured items that make baristas laugh and brighten my day," she says. If you bring a reusable cup, you can save as much as 50p on coffee in Pret A Manger and Starbucks. We recommend seeking out the sustainably-produced, leak-averse Frank Green range of reusable bottles and cups.

RETHINK FOOD

The real battleground is the supermarket. In Europe, "precyling" no-waste markets are ahead of the curve, eliminating rubbish before it's created. In Berlin, Original Unverpackt is committed to zero waste with customers decanting measures of grains, nuts and legumes from gravity bins into their own mesh totes and hessian sacks. In Spain, Ms Judit Vidal and Mr Iván Álvaro's 12 Granel stores have a similar feel of plastic puritanism. In the UK, the plastic-free Bulk Market in East London is leading the charge and Waitrose has extended its "Unpacked" trials after an overwhelmingly positive response.

When you're in the supermarket, check the recyclability of the packaging and avoid products contained in composite materials, such as sandwich boxes with plastic windows. As an alternative, shop locally; loose fruit and vegetables at your greengrocer are much cheaper than at the supermarket, and if you have the time and space, growing your own salads and herbs is a sustainable option. Almost 80 per cent of milk is sold in plastic containers, so order from the local farmer if it's practical, or campaign to bring back your milkman.

CHANGE YOUR HABITS

It may surprise you quite how widespread plastic is. Many teabags, for instance, are not entirely biodegradable, because they contain a polypropylene "skeleton". Choose loose tea instead. Thermoplastic paints, used on houses, create a plastic dust, so look for brands that use linseed oil or latex as binders. If you don't know what to do with the plastics you already have, get rid of them responsibly at a plastics processing yard such as Powerday. (It has outposts in Willesden, Brixton and Enfield.)

In the bathroom, use soap bars instead of handwash, and loo roll that is unpackaged or that has compostable packaging, such as Ecoleaf. Most wipes typically contain plastics, so a traditional all-cotton flannel is the eco-friendly alternative. Worse still, wipes contribute to the "fatbergs" in sewer systems. Last year, the largest on record was found under the streets of Whitechapel. It was the length of two football pitches – the more waste we produce, the more monsters we create.

4
UPDATE YOUR WARDROBE

Start with what you're wearing. Synthetic textiles can shed up to 700,000 microfibres with each wash. These have no problem escaping the confines of sewage treatment plants and they're often ingested by wildlife. They can then travel up the food chain until they are consumed by us.

Fortunately, there are alternatives and solutions. Stella McCartney and Nike have pledged support for the Ellen MacArthur Foundation's rethink on the textile economy, while adidas has collaborated with Parley For The Oceans for their adidas x Parley range. Biosteel, a German startup, creates artificial silk fibres and has also teamed up with adidas to produce a biodegradable sneaker.

A fruitier innovation is AgraLoop, a Los Angeles startup that uses waste from bananas, pineapples and sugar cane to create cellulose-based fibres for textile manufacture.

If you can't commit to a new wardrobe, find a washing machine with the right filter. Alternatively, the Cora Ball can be tossed into the wash to attract and collect fibres. The Guppyfriend, meanwhile, is a mesh bag that you wash your synthetic clothes in to reduce fibre breakage and trap fibres that do come away.

5
STOP SMOKING

Was your New Year's resolution to quit smoking? Stick at it, and not just for your lungs' sake. Cigarette butts are more of an environmental menace than you might imagine. The filters are made from cellulose acetate, a non-biodegradable plastic, and not paper, as many of us assume.

According to the Marine Conservation Society, several trillion cigarette ends enter the environment every year, where they're mistaken for food and eaten by marine animals. They've been found in the guts of whales, dolphins, seabirds and turtles, where they can cause inflammation of the animal's digestive system and occasionally, if they cause a blockage of the gut, even death.

Not only do they shed microfibres, but, once used, they give off high levels of toxins, including nicotine, cadmium, lead and arsenic, making them a potent ocean pollutant.

MEN AND THEIR HOMES

MR PORTER gets a tantalising glimpse into the characterful havens of these international creatives

MR NICK WOOSTER *fashion consultant*

Having worked for Ralph Lauren, Calvin Klein and Thom Browne, fashion consultant and street-style icon, Mr Nick Wooster's one-bedroom apartment in New York's West Village resembles an upmarket menswear boutique. Of course, this being Manhattan, the furniture does double duty. A vintage drinks cabinet stores T-shirts, the oven is full of sweaters, and two matching Ikea bookshelves artfully display the boots and shoes he can't fit in his impressively ordered but overspilling cupboards.

Forever travelling, Mr Wooster reckons that he clocks up close to 250,000 miles a year. "This is me arriving home after another overseas trip," he says. "I am a chronic over-packer, so I make use of every available inch just as I do in my apartment. It's a New Yorker's skill." Despite the close quarters, Mr Wooster remains besotted with his pied-à-terre and its surrounds. "The West Village has been my home on and off for 30 years, and I love how it retains the feel of local stores," he says. "My tailor, barber and shoemaker are all within 100ft of my door. I do not cook at home so Morandi's restaurant, which is also about 30 seconds away, is essentially an extension of my apartment." *Mr Dan Rookwood*

Opposite page: Mr Nick Wooster photographed in New York by Mr Bill Gentle

MR PATRICK JOHNSON *founder, P. Johnson*

"Not a bad view, is it?" Mr Patrick Johnson sips a coffee on his glass-fronted balcony overlooking Tamarama, nicknamed Glamarama by Sydneysiders, one of the world's most picturesque city beaches. "I run down for a swim most mornings – there's no better way to start the day," says the Australian tailor, who is renowned for understated and elegant, made-to-measure designs, rendered in soft and comfortable style.

Mr Johnson and his interior designer wife, Ms Tamsin Johnson, bought the beach house shortly after returning to Sydney following a stint in New York, ahead of the birth of their son. "Tam actually sketched the design for the house while she was in bed the day after Arthur was born," he says. His wife designed P Johnson's showrooms in Sydney, Melbourne, London and New York, too. "I'm very lucky to work with Tam," he says. "We have a very similar aesthetic." Their joint appreciation of calm and contemplation extends far beyond their serene home – Mr Johnson encourages everyone who works for him (including Hector, the family's docile British bulldog) to meditate for 20 minutes twice a day. *Mr Dan Rookwood*

Mr Patrick Johnson, photographed in Sydney by Mr Bill Gentle

MR YASUTO KAMOSHITA *founder, Camoshita*

Internationally regarded as one of Tokyo's most stylish men, Mr Yasuto Kamoshita is the creative director of Japan's leading can't-go-wrong purveyor of on- and off-duty attire – the multi-brand powerhouse, United Arrows. Mr Kamoshita, who grew up in Tokyo's Shitamachi (downtown) area, came of age when men's magazines such as *Popeye* were popularising this mythic view of mid-century American menswear. "Ivy League style is something spiritual to me," he says of his inspirational cornerstone. "People who adhere to it never look elsewhere."

As well as influencing his personal wardrobe and creative practice, the harmonious interplay of global designs is reflected in Mr Kamoshita's stunning home in Edogawa, east Tokyo. "The style is a mix of mid-century Western with Japanese traditions. I styled the interior so that I'm surrounded by beautiful objects. I received the *shodo* calligraphy art from my father. It's important for that reason, but I don't know what it says. In such an environment, there's a tension that influences the way you think and live. I might be at home, where I try to relax as much as I can, but I never want to appear rough." *Mr James Coulson*

Mr Yasuto Kamoshita, photographed in Tokyo by Mr Bill Gentle

MR MARTIN BRUDNIZKI *interior architect*

"I don't ever want to feel plainness," says acclaimed Swedish-born, interior architect Mr Martin Brudnizki, sipping espresso at his kitchen's central breakfast bar. "I've never believed in the minimal cube – I believe in detailing the cube." Feted for crafting luxuriantly eclectic interiors, Mr Brudnizki and his team at his eponymous studio cherry-pick elements from across la belle époque, Art Deco and mid-century modern. "We've had classicism, we've had modernism, minimalism and maximalism… and what's great about the present moment is that you can do whatever you want in design as long as you can back it up conceptually."

It is in this spirit that Mr Brudnizki designed his own space – the top floor of a Victorian mansion block, which he shares with his partner, Mr Jonathan Brook – setting up the rooms as pocket sanctums of sculpture, artworks, tchotchkes and textiles. "I like layers. You have the simple architecture and then you can layer things such as furniture, art and lighting. For instance, our bookcase is full of books, objects and photographs. These make a space a home. A home is about me – I can decompress here, but still feel I'm feeding my soul." *Mr Oli Stratford*

Mr Martin Brudnizki, photographed in London by Mr Dan Wilton

MR MITCH GLAZER *writer and producer*

Head northeast out of Los Angeles into the vast, dusty Mojave Desert, that windblown, sun-faded Hades. Beyond Pearblossom Highway, the hills to the left suddenly sharpen into tectonic teeth as, to the right, the land slopes into an alluvial marsh – now, you are almost at the Glazer house. "Psychologically, when you take that drive and hit Mojave, you're somewhere else," says lauded screenwriter, producer and director, Mr Mitch Glazer. The city falls away and "everything after that feels like an adventure. You end up somewhere lunar and extreme."

For 31 years, this spectacular outpost, built by Mr Richard Neutra in 1959, has been Mr Glazer's creative retreat – a place to dream his big-screen dreams. In that time, very little in this house has changed: the original canary-yellow laminate still covers the guest bathroom sink; the fascias on all the cupboards remain the same. "The amazing thing about this home is, when you try to put things in it, the house rejects them outright," says Mr Glazer. Little wonder he and his actor wife, Ms Kelly Lynch, feel a profound connection to the place. Still, amid these ancient boulders, Hollywood feels a million miles away. *Mr Chris Wallace*

Mr Mitch Glazer, photographed in Los Angeles by Mr Manfredi Gioacchini

MR RICK OWENS *designer*

The great American designer Mr Rick Owens has been coming to Venice regularly since he moved his manufacturing to Concordia, Italy, almost 15 years ago. In 2014, enchanted by the "most impractical, magical, legendary city ever", he committed to a permanent residence in the guise of a penthouse apartment atop his beloved Lido. To his partner, Ms Michèle Lamy's dismay, he promptly tore up the 1970s turquoise tile floor to lay down travertine marble – wall-to-wall, floor-to-ceiling marble.

But Mr Owens doesn't find this – nor his grand, brutalist furniture; nor 1930s Italian Futurist busts of Mr Benito Mussolini – to be at all uncomfortable. "I had a very severe formality in mind," he says of his home's concept. "But whenever I do that, there are huge places to sprawl, so it's all about reclining." The throne-shaped, black marble toilets are just about being thorough with the aesthetic: "I needed to create a space that was severe and avoided any kind of sentimentality or attachments, a blank slate to concentrate on listening to what I really want. After you've showered in a marble cube, you're going to aspire to something higher... something better. And I have to be at my very, very, best." *Mr Chris Wallace*

Mr Rick Owens, photographed in Venice by Mr Jean-Francois Jaussard

How to:

MAINTAIN
A PERFECTLY
ORGANISED
WARDROBE

Your wardrobe is not just a receptacle for clothes. It's a life's work of careful curation and, more importantly, conservation. To put it bluntly, if you care at all about what you wear, you should think carefully about how you store it. Or don't think at all, and do exactly what we advise overleaf.

THE GROUND RULES

Don't overcrowd

Items should have one or two fingers' worth of space between them, so it's easy to choose what you want and to avoid wrinkles. Stuffing and squeezing things to fit is a sign that you need more storage or – and, believe us, we don't say this lightly – fewer clothes.

Know when to hang

Yes, it looks lovely having all your things lined up, but you shouldn't automatically put everything on a hanger, even if you have the space. Knitwear, in particular, is prone to warp and lose its shape if it's left hanging. Fold it up and put it in a drawer instead.

Use vacuum bags

You can maximise wardrobe space by rotating your clothes throughout the year and storing out-of-season pieces in vacuum bags. Everything emerges wrinkle-free. We don't know the science of it, but why question the universe when it does something right?

Roll, don't fold

Japanese tidiness expert Ms Marie Kondo advocates rolling items such as T-shirts, trousers and even underwear, then stacking them vertically in your drawers so you can see everything at once. Even die-hard folders can't deny that this makes things much easier to find.

Look to lavender

The bane of every wardrobe is moths, those evil, night-borne guzzlers. There are various methods to keep them at bay, but the most pleasant of them is hanging small sacks of lavender from your hangers. Not only does this dissuade the winged beasts, it will impart a pleasing fragrance.

THE DETAILS

The multi-tiered hanger

Short on space? These clever contraptions are perfect for holding three or four pairs of trousers in the same space a regular hanger holds one. They're particularly useful for fine wool trousers, which drape neatly over each other without much fuss.

The garment bag

Where possible, store suits in garment bags, attached with detailed, informative labels to save you frantically unzipping each bag when trying to find something. NB Every suit you order from MR PORTER comes in one of our very own white garment bags. Just saying.

The drawer divider

Yes, you could spend hours fumbling around in that top drawer every morning, but the clever thing to do is install dividers, either off-the-shelf or custom-made. This way, even in the dark, you can get to the thing you need straight away, and every time.

The shoe tree

Any formal leather shoes should be stored on cedar shoe trees. This will help them keep their shape and slow the ageing process. Plus, as we know, moths aren't keen on cedar, which is a bonus.

The drop zone

Save a shelf in your wardrobe to store your work bag, if you have one, and make a point of keeping your wallet, keys and other essentials in it if you're not using them. That way, you won't have to scramble to assemble everything each morning.

9

GOING PLACES

HOW TO BOOK A HOLIDAY

Whether you're hoping to score
a room upgrade or simply avoid
the crowds, these travel hacks
will help you do it better

Words by Ms Jenny Southan

Marrakech or Mykonos? Design hotel in Chicago or chalet in Verbier?
Even frequent flyers deliberate when it comes to planning a well-
earned getaway. Whether you're trying to balance price with quality,
or convenience with curiosity, there are many variables to weigh up.
But, like painting or playing the flute – to take two completely random
examples – booking a holiday is something of an art form: you can do it
very well or very badly. However you approach the task, it always helps
to have a few tips and tricks up your sleeve, especially if you're working
a little in advance.

Over the page, you can find a selection of holiday-booking hacks
from architect Mr André Fu and hotelier Mr Guillaume Marly, alongside
seasoned travel editors, jet-setting PR gurus and, yes, your humble
author. Call upon these to make better decisions and get the most out of
your stay when you arrive. Bon voyage!

2

COMBINE YOUR HOTEL AND FLIGHT BOOKING

If you're looking for a good deal, try booking your hotel and flight through the same provider. British Airways, for example, allows you to add on accommodation, and even car rental and experiences, all in one go. Normally, you need to include a Saturday-night stay for this deal.

1

SPEAK TO A HUMAN

"If you're new to a property and looking for special treatment, call the hotel directly and speak to a human being," suggests Mr Guillaume Marly, managing director of Hotel Café Royal, London. "Tell them it's your first time, a special occasion, and you would be grateful for anything that can be done to make the experience more memorable. Be polite. Top-quality hotels are unlikely to offer discounts, but late check-outs, upgrades and extra amenities in the room are pretty common."

3

TRY "AFFORDABLE LUXURY" BRANDS

There is a growing trend for "affordable luxury" hotels that offer stylish interior design, chic communal spaces and top dining. Good examples include Life House, with three Miami properties, Mr Ian Schrager's Public hotel in New York, Marriott's Moxy, AccorHotels' Mama Shelter and 25hours, Dutch brand citizenM, and Ace Hotel's Sister City.

BE SPONTANEOUS

An app called One Night, created by Standard International, the parent company of Standard Hotels, offers a savvy way to nab affordable same-day stays at boutique hotels in US cities such as New York, Boston and Chicago, as well as London. (European expansion is planned.) Log on after 12.00pm on the day you want to stay and see what is available.

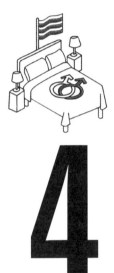

LOOK AT HOTEL COLLECTIONS

"I'm a big fan of hotel collections," says Mr Uwern Jong, editor-in-chief of *Out There* magazine. "Gay travellers, for example, are keen to know about hotels around the world that will be welcoming. Preferred Hotels and Resorts has a collection called Preferred Pride. These properties have all made a point of highlighting that they are LGBT-friendly and have undertaken sensitivity training."

OPT FOR SMALLER HOTELS

"Check the number of rooms the hotel has before booking," advises Mr André Fu, founder of design studio AFSO. "I'm a strong believer in staying in small to mid-size properties that have a more personal approach to hospitality and generally avoid hotels with over 300 rooms (this can be typical in the Asian market)."

7

NEVER BOOK THE
CHEAPEST ROOM

"Go up one or two levels and your
chance of an upgrade will increase
dramatically," advises Mr Philippe
Kjellgren, founder of luxury travel
club and app PK's List.

9

CONSIDER THE DATA

When planning a holiday, check out
Kayak's Travel Trends portal, which
uses data from 1.5 billion annual
searches to show which places
are most popular and when, and
provides expected price forecasts
for destinations across each month.
For example, if you're thinking
about travelling from London to
Bangkok, you can easily see that
December is the most expensive
time, while somewhere like Auckland
is cheapest in May.

8

ENLIST THE HELP
OF A TRAVEL AGENT

"A hotel manager once told me, those
who book through online travel agents
rarely get the best room, because
there is no incentive for management
to build loyalty with that price-driven
customer," says Mr Jong. "However,
if you book via a real-life travel agent,
creating a positive experience is
paramount, as the hotel will want to
ensure the agent continues to send
high-value customers its way. Agents
will be able to guarantee special
requests and better amenities."

10

SPLIT A HIGH-END RENTAL

For groups of friends, Parisian startup Le Collectionist offers a high-end alternative to Airbnb. From four-bedroom chalets in Courchevel to seven-bedroom villas in Mykonos, the properties are expensive, but can work out to be good value when split between a group of guests.

11

REQUEST A HUMIDIFIER

"I always request a humidifier for my room as the air in hotels can be so dry," says Ms Jo Vickers, founder of travel PR firm JV Public Relations. I also turn off the air-conditioning – this aids sleep. And if the windows open, this can help, too."

12

BOOK DURING SOFT OPENINGS

"Most hotels will go through a soft-opening period for anything from a couple of weeks to three months, and it's likely they will offer significantly reduced rates or special deals such as three nights for the price of two," says Mr Marly. "It's possible that not all the facilities will be open during this period, and the staff might still be getting to grips with all the systems, but the savings will be worth it."

UNPACKING COMMON PACKING MISTAKES

The contents of your bag can greatly improve the quality of your trip

Words by Mr Mansel Fletcher

Travel is enticing, but it can also be difficult. Whether it involves a plane, train or automobile, too often the reality is uncomfortable, demeaning and tiring. Somehow, the understandable sense that journeys are to be endured has come to inform our approach to packing.

It's true that there are some trips when time is of the essence, where the difference between travelling with a carry-on and checking in a bag could mean making – or missing – your meeting. On such occasions, there isn't much for it but to slip a clean shirt, socks and boxers into a soft briefcase and hope the person sitting next to you on the flight doesn't spill their drink in your lap. But this spartan approach to packing is a necessary evil rather than a blueprint to follow every time you travel.

The days when rich men travelled with a steamer trunk full of clothes may be over, but despite the democratisation of modern travel, the mantra of packing light has gone too far. It's not a disaster if you bring back an unworn item of clothing. Better to have had it and not needed it than to have needed it and not had it. Whether you're away for work or for pleasure, it's gratifying to be well-dressed in whatever situation you find yourself, and potentially uncomfortable to be found sartorially wanting.

Good packing can affect more than just your appearance. Packing really well (or not) can change the mood of your entire trip, but in order to achieve this you'll need to abandon some oft-repeated shibboleths about the right way to pack. Let's bust some of those myths.

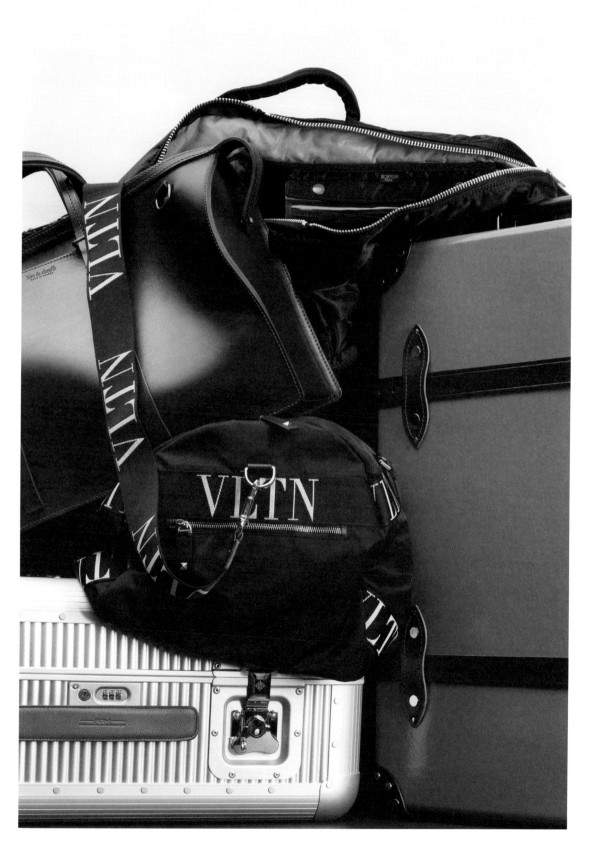

Myth: There's a perfect bag out there
Reality: Everyone needs a variety of bags

There's no such thing as the perfect bag, only the right bag for the trip you're about to undertake. When travelling light is paramount, a briefcase with room for a spare shirt and boxers is sufficient. If you must stick with carry-on luggage, then a small holdall offers greater flexibility and will look better than a small trolley case. When it comes to longer trips, it's helpful to consider the nature of your destination. If you're taking a lot of kit for an action-packed vacation, then a big, rugged holdall likely works best because of the additional capacity it can offer. Whereas if you're staying somewhere more sophisticated, then a suitcase will deliver your clothes with fewer wrinkles. In such circumstances the practical answer is a big trolley case, but men with stronger arms, and a keener concern for their image, should consider an old-fashioned suitcase.

Myth: No one uses hotel gyms
Reality: Business trips are a great opportunity to exercise

It's easy to give yourself entirely to the demands of a business trip and to adopt a work-hard, play-hard attitude. Better, we think, to claw back some valuable me-time in the form of a swim or a run either before the day's meetings begin or before dinner. It's probably no bad thing if, in order to be able to get up and exercise the following morning, you don't stay until the bitter end of the evening's entertainment. There are personal and professional advantages to keeping a clear head when you're away from home, and returning in better shape than you were before the trip is a worthwhile prize. To achieve this, check out the hotel's gym facilities in advance and pack some appropriate sportswear.

Myth: A man needs one set of clothes per day
Reality: Most men need to change their clothes twice each day

There's a pleasing simplicity to the idea that a guy needs a fresh shirt, socks and underwear each day. The reality is that he can only really claim to be civilised if he takes two sets of underclothes for every day of the trip. Whether you're sitting in stuffy meeting rooms, touring building sites or trekking in the forest, the clothes worn during the day need to go into the dirty laundry bag when you get back to the hotel for that pre-dinner shower, to be replaced with fresh garments.

Myth: Rolling clothes prevents them becoming creased in your bag
Reality: It's best to pack your clothes flat

The idea that rolling clothes stops them creasing en route has gained widespread acceptance. It's nonsense. No less an authority than Savile Row tailor Mr Thomas Mahon says that rolling clothes simply increases the number of creases. He counsels that clothes be packed horizontally, with as few folds as possible. Where you do have to fold tailored clothes, put something soft (such as a pair of rolled boxer shorts) inside the crease so that it's not crushed flat. Make sure you hang your clothes up as soon as you get into your hotel room. Jackets constructed from high-twist wool should spring back well, while linen clothes and suits made from very fine fabrics have a notoriously long memory when it comes to wrinkles.

Myth: It's best to pack a versatile selection of clothes in bland colours
Reality: Outfits, not clothes, are the way forward

When you're at home, you can easily pull together a formal outfit from the contents of your wardrobe. When travelling, you have to work with a restricted collection. There are two ways around this problem. The first is to make sure all the elements work together by taking only white shirts, blue suits and grey trousers on a business trip. The more enjoyable alternative is to pack outfits, having figured them out at home in advance. Lay out a full ensemble for each day you're away (you can wear some of these garments more than once). Your only limit is the number of shoes you can take with you. Take a phone snap of each outfit so that, even if you're jet-lagged, you can remember what to put on every morning.

Myth: The smartphone provides all the in-flight entertainment you need
Reality: Not even Apple has made reading redundant (yet)

Whisper it, but we make a harsh judgement when we see a grown man occupying himself with *Candy Crush* on a plane or train. The obvious alternative source of entertainment is mind-numbing social media feeds, but it's surely better to make the most of your journey's hang time by reading. Whether you're in the mood for self-improvement from someone such as Mr Tony Robbins, the latest page-turner by some gloomy Scandinavian author, or a much admired tome from the canon, take a book with you. And for those moments when you're too tired to read, we strongly recommend a podcast.

THE FOUR BEST
ECO-RESORTS
ON THE PLANET

The most sustainable places
to recharge your batteries and
salve your conscience

Words by Mr Simon Usborne

LA GRANJA *Ibiza (opposite)*

Rarely is the environmental cost of simply living more starkly drawn than when we go on holiday. There is zero point in denying the heft of our carbon footprint as we plod on to planes and through grand hotels' air-conditioned corridors. Still, there is cheer to be found in the rising trend for conscientious spaces where eco and luxe truly co-exist.

Few Balearic locales rival the green and serene credentials of La Granja. The sprawling 16th-century farmstead has been transformed into a members-only retreat by Design Hotels with Friends Of A Farmer, an arty agricultural movement. The rustic-luxe hideaway comprises a large farmhouse, standalone guesthouse and a pool that looks out over produce-rich, terraced fields. La Granja works with the Ibiza Preservation Fund to help safeguard the island's natural and agricultural heritage and offers guests yoga, biodynamic farming and slow-food workshops.

SAFFIRE FREYCINET *Australia*

When it opened on Tasmania's mountainous east coast in 2010, the Saffire Freycinet's unrivalled cooking and service shook up Australia's luxury lodge market. Resembling a beached stingray from above, its collection of 20 suites, linked via a walkway to the main lodge, still attracts awards today. And, as more than 30,000 native plants reach maturity in its protected grounds, the giant structure increasingly blends in between the granite Hazards mountains behind and the ocean views across Coles Bay. The hotel is dedicated to sustainability and does everything from limiting light pollution to composting. Beyond it, Freycinet National Park features Wineglass Bay beach and plays host to Tasmanian possums and the lesser-known, long-nosed potoroo.

MARATABA TRAILS LODGE *South Africa*

Deep within South Africa's northernmost Limpopo Province, the Waterberg massif was once overlooked among the region's great wildernesses. Yet with the creation of the Marakele National Park, a vast reserve in which the luxury Marataba Safari and Trails Lodges have a private concession, it claimed its place on the safari map. The site's five deluxe eco-suites are solar powered (the lodge is totally off-grid) and boast sweeping views of the river below and nearby escarpment. The central lodge has a pool that looks over the towering cycads and cedars, which are home to colonies of birds, including Cape vultures. Game tours offer sightings of resurgent populations of big cats, elephants and rhinos.

TIERRA PATAGONIA *Chile*

From the infinity pool at the Tierra, a hotel and architectural statement on the shores of Patagonia's breathtakingly blue Lake Sarmiento, bathers may gaze out at the snow-capped towers of the Torres del Paine massif as they punch into the sky like great, granite fists. The work of Chilean architect Ms Cazú Zegers, the understated, S-shaped hotel is clad in washed lenga wood. During construction, all surrounding vegetation was preserved so it could be replanted, and the building is now frequented by llama-like guanacos and flightless birds called ñandús. Inside, towering windows frame those jaw-dropping panoramas. Just 15 minutes away, Torres del Paine National Park offers further hiking and gawping opportunities.

315

THE PEOPLE TO AVOID AT THE AIRPORT

From Mr Business to Mr Lad-On-Tour, the five archetypes you can expect to encounter next time you're cashing in your air miles

Words by Mr Chris Elvidge

If you were an alien visiting Earth and you had only a single day to learn as much as you could about the human race, what would you do? Visit an art gallery? Attend a political rally? Become an Uber driver? If it were us, we'd head directly and without hesitation to the departure hall of our nearest major international airport. They may not seem the most natural habitat in which to observe human behaviour – modern ones in particular, with their antiseptic surfaces of steel and glass, hardly look as if they were built to sustain life – but airports play host to as broad a sample of humanity as you're likely to find anywhere on the planet.

Of course, what unites those making up this hotbed of diversity is that no one actually wants to be there. Unlike the crowds drawn to a sports game or music festival, the only thing that the transient denizens of an airport have in common is a fervent desire to get out as soon as possible. In that sense, the airport is a great leveller. It breaks down social barriers, throwing people together from all walks of life. And hidden within this human tapestry, there are a few classic stereotypes you are almost certain to encounter. Below, we take you through five of the worst offenders.

MR FIRST CLASS

This guy hops on and off planes like
rabbits hop on and off... well, each
other. So while you're adjusting your
tie knot and practising your best
"Hey, I was just wondering if there
were any empty seats in business"
smile in the bathroom mirror, he's
rolling out of an airport lounge so
exclusive that you don't even know
it exists. Dressed in the standard
C-level executive off-duty outfit
of cashmere tracksuit, baseball
cap, slides and socks – so much
smoother at security – and with his
$500 noise-cancelling headphones
carefully tuned to block out the
world, he looks like an overgrown,
expensively dressed teenager who
just rolled out of bed. Not that it
matters, though, because unlike
you, he has no doubt about which
way he's turning when he gets on the
plane. In fact, he probably knows
which seat he's sitting in, the vintage
of the champagne that's waiting
to be uncorked on his arrival, and
the first name – and star sign – of
the air hostess who'll be personally
attending to him throughout the
flight. No wonder he looks so smug.

MR LAD-ON-TOUR

Yep, there's always one. The "it's past noon somewhere in the world!" excuse might pass muster with the barman – who, just to clarify, is being paid to be nonjudgemental – but that fourth pint of lager certainly isn't impressing the young family trying to eat breakfast at the next table. To be fair to our early-doors boozer, the rules of etiquette governing when it is and isn't OK to drink can seem a little contradictory at times. Especially when you happen to be drunk. Like, why is it definitely not OK to crack open a beer at 7.00am, but it's *kind of* OK if you haven't been to bed yet? And if it's normal to have a glass of wine with lunch in France, does that mean you can have a shot of tequila, too? Also, why do your brunch pals look so concerned when you try to order a vodka and Coke with your eggs florentine, but if you order a Bloody Mary, they tell you to put it on Instagram? Valid questions, all, and ones for which we cannot provide a definite answer. What we can tell you, though, is that in moments of uncertainty it is wise to err on the side of caution. Or, in other words, just because you *can* drink doesn't mean that you *should*. Have some dignity, man.

MR EAGER BEAVER

Anyone who has been to an airport before knows that the suggested minimum arrival time – three hours before your flight is due to take off – is only there to ensure that you spend as much time as possible in duty-free buying things that you neither want nor need. This guy clearly didn't get the memo. Either that, or he just really loves airports. Specifically, queueing at airports. And it isn't enough for him to be first through check-in: no, he also needs to be first at the gate, first on the plane (thanks to Speedy Boarding Ultra Plus), first to stash his carry-on in the overhead storage locker, first to take it back out again, first at the luggage carousel... It's almost as if he's short on time. But if that's the case, then why did he show up to the airport 180 minutes early?

MR BUSINESS

You know those guys who didn't realise that *American Psycho* was a satire on consumerism and corporate greed? The ones who decided immediately after watching it to pursue a career in investment banking because, well, it all looks so super-glamorous and fun? Well, this guy did something similar – only he was watching *Up In The Air*. This 2009 comedy-drama follows the life of Ryan Bingham, a corporate hatchet man who spends his life jetting back and forth across the US sacking people. Bingham, played by Mr George Clooney, has become something of a role model among image-conscious business travellers, who see in his peripatetic life of luxury something deeply aspirational – so much so that they're willing to ignore the fact that he is clearly a deeply unfulfilled man. Just so we're clear, guys: a 10-million-mile air miles account is not necessarily a sign of a life well lived. You'll be able to recognise Mr Business by his sleek carry-on luggage, his immaculately turned-out appearance – oh, and the thousand-yard stare of his cold, dead eyes.

MR ANGRY

"Look, sir. I understand. Of course I do. Nobody likes having to remove their shoes in order to satisfy the arbitrary legal requirements of an under-qualified airport official. No, I've never personally seen a bomb hidden in a brogue, but I'm assured it has happened before. No, sir, that 125ml moisturiser that you forgot to check in with your main bag probably isn't stuffed with Semtex, either, but we still have to dispose of it. I'm afraid it's just policy. I haven't heard of 'La Mer'. Yes, I'm sure it is expensive. No, sir, you don't look like a terrorist to me, but if you keep saying 'terrorist' and 'bomb', you're going to alarm the other passengers. Please remove your shoes, sir. I won't ask again. No, I don't have a shoe horn."

UPGRADE YOUR TRAVEL WARDROBE

Globetrotters from Mr Theo Hutchcraft to Mr Eric Underwood reveal their go-to travel outfits and tips for a smooth journey

Words by Mr Tom M Ford

Travel often brings out the worst in our wardrobes. Next time you're in an airport, take a moment at check-in to look around. What do you see? Holidaymakers in saggy sweats and neck supports, and pasty men dressed like Mr Hunter S Thompson. Hawaiian shirts and shorts may look great in St Barts, but in Luton? Not so much.

We asked five men with more air miles under their Italian belts than most to tell us how they travel in style. From a globe-trotting pop star to a creative CEO, they reveal what to wear, how to pack and also share their insider travel tips (eg, never take a sleeping pill before the plane actually takes off – find out why from MR PORTER Contributing Fashion Editor Mr Dan May). Before you check in for your next flight, check out their advice.

Mr Eric Underwood

Left: Mr Dan May. *Above*: Mr Theo Hutchcraft

THE FLEXIBLE FLYER

Mr Eric Underwood, Royal Ballet soloist and model
Fresh from performing in a matinee at the Royal Opera House in London, Mr Eric Underwood, who was born in Washington DC, arrives on our shoot with an energy that belies the fact he has another performance afterwards. Mr Underwood's work ("How did I get into ballet? I failed at an acting audition") has taken him to St Petersburg, Italy and California.

Why did you pick this look?
I always need to be ready for that "hello" from the person I didn't expect to see at the airport. I have to change clothes a lot in my line of work, so when I travel, I want to throw on something easy, but not old sweatpants. I love this shirt because it has a beautiful pattern, but it's also flowy, so I feel comfortable. I could wear it to dinner, lunch or an after-performance drink.

What essentials do you travel with?
A great pair of sneakers. A pair of wonderful dark jeans. You can throw them on with anything and get going. And my phone charger.

What's the worst thing that has happened on a trip?
I went on a work trip to Mexico. I was performing on stage and my pants fell down to my ankles. I stood in front of thousands of people with just a G-string on. It was a nightmare. I picked them up as elegantly as possible.

THE COOL CUSTOMER

Mr Theo Hutchcraft, lead singer of Hurts
We meet Yorkshire-born Mr Theo Hutchcraft shortly after the release of *Surrender,* his band's acclaimed third album. "It was the most fun we've ever had making an album," he says. "From LA to Switzerland to New York to Ibiza, the whole process was made up of travelling." We ask him how, as a globally recognised musician, he keeps things neat when he's constantly on the move.

Why did you choose this look?
Normally, I wear trousers that are smart versions of tracksuits. I find jeans so uncomfortable. A good coat is crucial. You can wear it to save space in your luggage, for when we arrive in, say, Eastern Europe, in the middle of winter. Also, we often have a lot of fans waiting for us, so you have to think about presentation.

How do you like to pack?
I've spent my life working out how little I can take to places when I travel, so I just have one bag. I've also got a Berluti cotton suit carrier, which weighs nothing and goes over my shoulder. I can put a jacket, trousers and shirt in it.

Any other tips?
I take a book rather than my computer, so I'm not able to do much work, and I feel like I'm on holiday. I always sit near the front of the plane, by the aisle. There's more leg room and you're on and off the plane straightaway. Oh, and don't queue up to get on the plane. Just sit down and chill.

THE PRACTICAL PASSENGER

Mr Dan May, Contributing Fashion Editor, MR PORTER
With more than 25 years' styling experience, Mr Dan May is more comfortable behind a camera than posing in front of one. Required to be on a plane "every other week" for his work, Mr May dresses with practicality in mind.

Why did you choose this look?
I'm not one of these "fashion" people. I need to be comfortable for my job, because I'm lifting things, bending down and pinning, and generally running around. When I'm getting on a plane, I prefer to wear tracksuit bottoms, so I don't have to go to the loo to put on a sleeper suit. I can just rest for a couple of hours, put my shoes back on, slip on a jacket and I'm ready to go and work.

Does any particular piece stand out?
Wearing a travel blanket as a chunky scarf, like this one by Armand Diradourian – cashmere, obviously – is a bit of a signature for me.

Give us a travel tip.
Wait until you've taken off before you take a sleeping pill. Once, I took it too early, passed out and had to be shaken awake because there was a problem with the plane. I was virtually in a coma.

How does one get bumped up to first class?
When I'm checking in, I always look at the staff to see who seems like they're in a good mood. I'll hang back and pick the person who's smiling.

Left: Mr Rich Stapleton. *Above*: Mr Gwyn Jones

THE LONG-HAUL EXPERT

Mr Rich Stapleton, creative director of Cereal *magazine*
Mr Stapleton launched his influential, travel-focused publication in
December 2012 with his partner, Ms Rosa Park. Based in Bath, he spends
half his year in far-flung locations.

Why does this outfit work for travelling?
On planes, they always blast the air conditioning. I usually wear a
chunky knit and some thick cords or sweats, so I can get up and do a bit
of stretching. In transit, you can relax and snuggle into your big, thick
cardigan. And when you arrive at the hotel, you still look presentable.

What are your top three travel essentials?
I take a film camera, such as a Canon A-1, so I can document the trip.
I always pack a scarf, even if I'm going to a tropical destination. Third?
A portable fragrance such as a Le Labo Santal 33 Travel Tube.

Do you have a trip that is particularly memorable?
We went to the Sahara desert in Morocco a few years ago on a shoot for
the magazine. We were the only people as far as the eye could see.

THE BUSINESS-CLASS TRAVELLER

Mr Gwyn Jones, chairman of Quill Content
Chairman of Quill, a content creator for businesses, Mr Gwyn Jones is
a well-travelled creative professional. He combines smart clothes with
casual and knows "the routines for making travel as painless as possible".

What travel tips can you give us?
Don't wear your 18-hole Dr. Martens to go through security. Go with loafers,
and you're in and out quickly. The cabin temperature seems to drop after
take-off, so take a sweater such as a John Smedley merino wool crewneck.

Tell us about the outfit you chose today.
I can do very casual clothes, but not that "middle" wardrobe. So, when
I'm getting on a plane, I wear jeans, a T-shirt and a jacket.

Any other travel essentials?
I find my mind wanders, so I use a notepad to record my thoughts. And to
avoid bed hair, I take one of Pankhurst London's products for a quick fix.

How to:

DRESS FOR
LONG-HAUL TRAVEL

Whoever came up with the hoary old cliché that it's the journey and
not the destination that counts has obviously never flown long-haul
in economy. The days when members of the jet set flew from one exotic
idyll to another in airplanes that resembled five-star hotels are well
and truly over. Perhaps one day someone such as Mr Elon Musk will
invent a *Star Trek*-esque teleportation machine to get us to the beach
in Bali or the business meeting in New York at the mere press of
a button. But until that time, we're going to have to rely on the
following tips to get us from A to B in style.

THE GROUND RULES

Dress adaptively

When moving between countries, through airports and wrangling with the intermittently frigid or roasting conditions of never-quite-properly air-conditioned aircraft cabins, you're going to experience extremes of temperature. The only way to prepare is by wearing lots of light, easily removable layers, which can be peeled off or piled on as you need.

Strip back the accessories

There are few things more annoying than waiting your turn at airport security while the passenger in front of you fumbles to liberate himself from his belt, watch, cufflinks and other metals. So, be kind to others – if you don't absolutely need these items for the duration of your flight (and why would you?), it's best to omit them from your travelling outfit.

Pack a washbag

But not just any washbag. Yes, you'll want to brush your teeth after idly wolfing down whatever in-flight meal is dumped in front of you. But you should be also kind to your skin, because, at 30,000 feet, there is not only less moisture in the air, but a higher concentration of UV rays. Cleanse and moisturise during the flight and consider an anti-pollution spray.

Organise your carry-on

Obvious, perhaps, but worth saying – pack your carry-on bag so that the items you need during the flight (your wash bag, for example) are on top. We recommend any bag with a front pocket that's big enough to hold your passport – put it there, keep it there, and return it there whenever you don't need it. That way, there's no need for any pocket-patting.

Be decent, won't you?

There's a certain type of traveller who shows up dressed as if for a *Game Of Thrones* marathon, in a tank top, sweats, slippers and such. Don't be that person. It's important to be comfortable, but also to consider the proprieties of the several hundred people you'll be squished into close proximity with. They don't need to see your bare shoulders or feet.

THE DETAILS

The neck pillow

They can be cumbersome to lug around pre-flight, but trust us, if you're flying economy or premium, you need one of these. Airport shops can be dicey so seek yours out before. If you want to be flash, you can get a cashmere one – just don't leave it on the seat when you pop off to ask for more sour cream and chive pretzels.

The zip-up sweater

This is your warmth-giving layer in case someone flips the in-flight air-conditioning to the double snowflake symbol. It should have a zip fastening because you need to wriggle into it in a very tight space. In the summer, try a linen-cotton knit mix, and in winter go for cashmere – this will provide maximum warmth with minimum bulk.

The drawstring trousers

Yes, when you're flying, you can wear sweatpants rather than chinos or jeans. But a happy medium between the two – especially if you need to leap off the plane straight into a meeting or event – is a pair of loose-fitting drawstring trousers in a woven stretch cotton or shell fabric.

The slip-on sneakers

Choose shoes that can be taken on and off easily, such as slip-on sneakers. There is now a slip-on shoe for almost every occasion, so you won't need to sacrifice style for practicality – especially important if you're travelling for business. Look to Vans or Common Projects for slip-on sneakers that are hardy and lightweight. The Balenciaga Speed Sock is a slip-on that is enviably stretchy, making it a great travel companion.

The luggage

Your luggage says as much about you as its contents. The North Face signals eco credentials while the classicism of Globe-Trotter shows you pine for a more civilised era of travel. Overnight trip? Try to fit everything in a backpack. A holdall works for a weekend break and a long-haul case should have a hard shell to protect your belongings.

ACKNOWLEDGEMENTS

Brand & Content Director
Mr Jeremy Langmead

Creative Direction and Design
B.A.M.

Editors
Ms Suze Olbrich, Mr Chris Wallace, Mr Adam Welch

Sub-Editors
Mr Jim Merrett, Ms Roni Omikorede

Picture Director
Ms Katie Morgan

Production
Ms Xanthe Greenhill, Ms Rachael Smart, Ms Lucy Thorp

MR PORTER Creative Director
Mr Ben Palmer

Special thanks
Ms Fedora Abu, Ms Michelle Corps, Mr Colin Crummy,
Mr Jonathan Dann, Mr Chris Elvidge, Ms Lili Göksenin,
Ms Clementine Hart-Walsh, Ms Cathy Levy, Ms Emily
Lucas, Mr Anish Patel, Mr John Ortved, Ms Catherine
Small, Mr Gareth Watkins, Ms Claire Wilson

CREDITS

249 Photograph by Mr Victor Bockris/Corbis via Getty Images
250 Photograph by Keystone USA via ZUMA PRESS
251 Photograph by Mondadori Portfolio via Getty Images
252 Photograph by Gunther/MPTV Images
253 Photograph by NY Daily News Archive via Getty Images
254 Illustration by Ms Elena Xausa
259 Illustration by Mr Ferry Gouw
268 Illustration by Ms Elena Xausa
271–273 Illustrations by Ms Elena Xausa
275–280 Photographs by Mr Norman Wilcox-Geissen
275–280 Styling by Ms Lianna Fowler
282–285 Illustrations by Ms Elena Xausa
295 Illustration by Mr Ferry Gouw
301–305 Illustrations by Ms Elena Xausa
307–311 Photographs by Mr Norman Wilcox-Geissen
307–311 Styling by Ms Lianna Fowler
313 Photograph courtesy of Design Hotels™
315 (top) Photograph courtesy of Saffire Freycinet; (middle) photograph
courtesy of The MORE Family Collection; (bottom) photograph by
Mr James Florio, courtesy of Tierra Patagonia
317–319 Illustrations by Ms Elena Xausa
320–327 Photographs by Mr Brendan Freeman
331 Illustration by Mr Ferry Gouw

MR PORTER is the global online retail destination for men's style, offering more than 550 of the world's leading menswear brands.

What MR PORTER.COM can do you for you:

Worldwide delivery within 72 hours
Free style advice from our Style Advisors
You have up to four weeks to arrange returns and exchanges
We're happy to collect them from your home or office for free
24-hour customer care, seven days a week

Visit us at MR PORTER.COM

Email styleadvice@mrporter.com or call 0800 044 5706 from the UK, +44(0)203471 4092 from Europe, Asia, the Middle East and Australia. From the US, email styleadvice.usa@mrporter.com or call +1 877 95 77 677. Style Advisors are available between 9.00am − 5.00pm BST and EST, Monday to Friday

Published in the United Kingdom in 2020 by Thames & Hudson Ltd
181A High Holborn, London WC1V 7QX by arrangement with Net-A-Porter Group Ltd

The MR PORTER Guide To A Better Day © 2020 Net-A-Porter Group Ltd

British Library Cataloguing-in-Publication Data
A catalogue record for this book is available from the British Library
ISBN 978-0-500-29570-0

Printed and bound in China by C & C Offset Printing Co. Ltd

To find out about all our publications, please visit *www.thamesandhudson.com*.
There you can subscribe to our e-newsletter, browse or download our current
catalogue, and buy any titles that are in print.